NETA LOHNES FRAZIER

STOUT-HEARTED SEVEN
THE TRUE ADVENTURE OF THE SAGER CHILDREN ORPHANED ON THE OREGON TRAIL IN 1844

Northwest Interpretive Association   ⁓   Seattle, Washington

Printed in the United States of America by the Northwest Interpretive Association, a non-profit corporation managed by a Board of Directors. Its purpose is to provide for the enhanced enjoyment and understanding of visitors to its areas of operation in the states of Washington, Oregon, Idaho, Montana, and California.

Published by: Northwest Interpretive Association
909 First Avenue, Suite 630
Seattle, WA 98104-3627
206-220-4140
www.nwpubliclands.com

Cover and Interior Design: Mark MacKay
Cover photograph: © 2002 Jeff Gnass

Library of Congress Cataloging in Publication Data

Frazier, Neta (Lohnes) 1890-1990
    Stout-hearted seven.

    SUMMARY: Recounts the adventures of the seven Sager children during their journey to Oregon where they were adopted by Marcus and Narcissa Whitman.
1.   Sager Family - Juvenile literature. [1. Sager family- Fiction.
2. Oregon Trail - Fiction]
I. Title
PZ7.F87Stt   [Fic]   73-5420
ISBN 0-914019-22-8

FOREWORD

—

Many children lost their parents on the journey across the plains during the westward migrations of the last century. Of them all, however, only this one family, the children of Henry and Naomi Sager, were taken into the home of the missionary couple Dr. Marcus Whitman and his wife, Narcissa, and thus became a part of United States history.

For three years, until the massacre of November 29, 1847, that brought the Oregon Mission of the Presbyterian and Congregational churches to a crashing end, these seven children knew the famous couple in a way no one else ever did, simply as father and mother.

The comfortable home at Waiilatpu (*Wy-eél-at-poo*) on the Walla Walla River, just over the Blue Mountains of Oregon, offered the weary emigrants food, rest, and medical assistance, enabling hundreds of men, women, and children to survive the final stage of the journey to the Willamette Valley. The Whitmans thus contributed to the influx of American settlers, which, in turn, swung the sovereignty of the Pacific Northwest to the United States instead of Great Britain.

For this service, Marcus Whitman, in sculptured form, stands as the representative of the State of Washington in Statuary Hall, Washington, D.C. This same service made him, to the Indians, the symbol of forces seeking to displace and destroy them, hence their arch enemy. The seven children, caught with their foster parents in the web of misunderstanding on which the mission had been founded and in the Indians' disappointment and rage, suffered with them the inevitable consequences of the clash of cultures that followed.

Several novelists, in writing the Sager story, have wandered so far from the truth as to have the children abandoned on the Oregon Trail after the deaths of their parents and forced to walk (barefoot, one three years old, one with a broken leg) the five hundred miles through the sagebrush desert of southern Idaho and over the Blue Mountains to the Whitman Mission, the older boy carrying the four-month-old infant and dragging the cow behind him.

Obviously, no such ridiculous thing was possible nor did it happen. Far from being abandoned, the Sager children were practically adopted by the members of the wagon train and tenderly escorted to the Whitman home. They and their descendants, down to the present time, have always cherished the memory of these kindly persons.

To tell the true story of the Sager children, as nearly as possible, has been my purpose in writing this book. I have gone back to primary sources: Catherine's *My Story*, in manuscript form; Matilda's book, *A Survivor's Recollections of the Whitman Massacre*, published by Esther Reed Chapter, Daughters of the American Revolution, Spokane, Washington; Elizabeth's interviews published from time to time in the *Oregon Journal* and *Oregon Spectator*, Portland, Oregon; and diaries of other members of the 1844 wagon train, published in *Transactions of the Oregon Pioneers' Association*, Portland. Added to these were the letters of Narcissa and Marcus Whitman, published in many volumes of the *Oregon*

Historical Quarterly, and in books written by Dr. Clifford M. Drury and published by the Arthur H. Clark Company, Glendale, California. Finally, and most useful, was personal information given me by two of Catherine's granddaughters, my friends Sadie Collins Armin, Sioux Falls, South Dakota, and Celista Collins Platz, Seattle, Washington.

Except for the necessary invention of dialogue and scenes, and an occasional shift in sequence to satisfy the needs of the story, all events in the book were related by one or more of the sisters, by the Whitmans, or by other contemporary persons, in conversations, letters, or diaries.

I am indebted to the library of Whitman College, Walla Walla, Washington, for use of its valuable collection of Sager letters and other documents; to the Spokane Public Library and the library of the Eastern Washington State Historical Society, Spokane, for access to their reference files; to the Oregon Historical Society, Portland, Oregon, and the Portland *Oregonian* for permission to see materials in their possession.

I am specially indebted to the members of the Spokane Writers for critical assistance throughout the writing of the book.

To all of these, my hearty thanks.

NETA LOHNES FRAZIER
Spokane, Washington, 1984

NETA LOHNES FRAZIER

STOUT-HEARTED SEVEN

THE TRUE ADVENTURE OF THE SAGER CHILDREN
ORPHANED ON THE OREGON TRAIL IN 1844

CHAPTER ONE

Catherine woke to the sound of fire crackling and the pleasant smell of wood smoke. She raised her head enough to look across the room to the big fireplace where Papa stood shaving strips from a stick onto the coals from yesterday's fire that had been covered with ashes through the night. Then he laid on bigger pieces, and the blaze leaped up in a burst of flame that sent pink shadows wavering over the pine ceiling above her head. She lay back to watch the color come and go.

Somehow the ceiling looked strange. So did the rest of the room. Now she remembered. This was not the house where she had lived for most of her eight and a half years, that everyone in Platte County, Missouri, knew as the Sager house. Her father, Henry Sager, her mother, Naomi, and the six children had moved over here yesterday, five miles from St. Joseph, near the Missouri River. She remembered the lovely red and gold leaves on the ground and the deep blue of the sky. "The most beautiful time of the year," Mama said.

Papa said they must always remember this fall of 1843 when they started for Oregon. They could not go on across the plains and mountains until next spring, but this was a start on their journey, and how lucky they were to be able to rent this cozy log house for the winter.

Oregon! Catherine lay back to think about it. What would it be like? Her brother Frank, who loved to tease, whispered stories of Indians lurking in the woods. Remembering his tales, Catherine shivered and drew the blanket over her face, for she feared Indians more than anything else in the world.

She heard the squeaking of the cords that supported the straw tick in the other big bed, then the sound of Mama padding across the bare floor in her old red and yellow carpet slippers. The door creaked open, letting in a whiff of cold, fresh air. That was Papa, going out for a pail of water from the well. She heard the splash as he poured it into the black kettle that hung on the crane over the fire.

"Frosty outside," he said. "We moved just in time to get settled in before winter."

Papa stepped across the room to the foot of the ladder leading up to the loft where his two sons slept. "John, Frank, time to get up. John, you go milk Bossy while your mother cooks breakfast. Frank, hustle down here and bring in your wood and water."

Catherine uncovered one eye to look at her brothers. They said they were not afraid of Indians; they wanted to go to Oregon. John's pleasant, round face appeared untroubled as he lifted the milk pail from a hook on the wall. At thirteen and a half, he was almost as tall as Papa. His straight brown hair hung into his eyes. Frank's hair was long, too, but appeared shorter because it curled in ringlets all over his head. With his pink cheeks and curls, he looked babyish even at eleven.

If only she could have curly hair like Frank's, thought Catherine. She and her sisters—Elizabeth, six; Matilda, four; and Louise, two and a half—were all small for their ages and looked as much alike as four peas in a pod, Papa said: little round faces; fine, straight, light hair; and grayish-blue eyes that nobody ever noticed. Everyone noticed Frank's eyes, which were the lively blue of April skies.

2

"I'll go feed the oxen." Papa tramped out after the boys. Catherine watched him cross the room, a stocky man of medium height, with thick, stubby brown hair and a short brown beard that Matilda loved to stroke as she sat on his lap. He had twinkly blue eyes and was always ready to laugh. Catherine loved his big, clever hands, which were equally capable whether he was wielding his blacksmith tools or soothing a sick child.

Papa was proud of his two yoke of oxen, Jake and Ike, Buck and Barney, perhaps because he had never owned oxen before. Next spring, he said, he would buy four more so they would have plenty of spares to pull their big covered wagon to Oregon.

Mama came over to the bed where Catherine, Elizabeth, and Matilda were snuggled in together. She was small but pretty, with her light brown hair neatly brushed and twisted into a knot at the top of her head, her cheeks pink from the fire, and her gray eyes sparkling. She turned back the covers. "Now then, chicks, while Papa and the boys are outside, you may come over near the fire to dress."

Matilda and Elizabeth burrowed deeper into the feather bed, but Louise, who slept in the cradle between the two big beds, sat up at once and demanded, "Up! up!"

"Wait a few minutes, Louise. Sister will dress you as soon as she can."

Catherine struggled into her clothes and took Louise on her lap. She could not remember a time when she had not been dressing or undressing babies. Not that she minded it too much, for she loved every one of them, but Elizabeth might help sometimes. Elizabeth, though, was awkward with buttons and buttonholes, and before she had done the last one of her own, Catherine had finished both Louise and Matilda.

The good smell of coffee filled the room as Mama bent over the fire, stirring the breakfast mush bubbling in the big, black iron kettle. Catherine led the two smallest girls to the washbench by the door, scrubbed their faces briskly, brushed their baby-fine hair back from their faces, and tied strips of blue calico around their heads. The bows on top looked almost as pretty as the ribbons they wore on Sundays. "Go give Mama a kiss," she commanded.

She and Elizabeth brushed their own hair, and each braided the other's pigtails. Then they, too, went to kiss Mama. She hugged them up close. "My helpers. What would I do without you? Now all slide into your places. Papa will be here in a minute."

The children sat on benches at each side of the table. Papa and Mama had chairs at the ends. While they waited, Catherine looked around the one room of their new house. The two beds at the end and the long table down the center almost filled it. Mama's cherrywood chest, her dearest possession, was pushed against the wall next to the ladder.

"Where will you put your loom, Mama?" Catherine asked.

"We can squeeze it in beside the window."

Papa had wanted to leave the loom behind. "You know we can't take it to Oregon," he had said.

"I know, but I want to use it this winter," had been Mama's reply.

He had grumbled a bit because he had to take it all apart to get it into the wagon, but he had done it. When Mama insisted, he almost always did what she wanted, but he would not yield about their going to Oregon. He had wanted to go last spring when he heard that the missionary Dr. Marcus Whitman was guiding emigrants across the plains. But Matilda was sick with a strange lump on one knee, so he had to give up his plan.

All that spring, while wagons passed their farmhouse every day, taking people to St. Joseph to start across the plains, Papa had worked over Matilda's knee. Friends called him Dr. Sager, though he was not a real doctor like Dr. Whitman. His father and grandfather had been skilled in caring for sick folks and had taught him all they knew. For a wedding present, his father had given him Dr. Gunn's book, *The Family Doctor*, which told all about every kind of sickness and what to do for it, and people were always coming to him for help.

By midsummer Matilda had been well again, but then Papa said it was too late to go to Oregon that year. Mama said that was good; she did not want to go at all.

Catherine remembered the day, only a few weeks ago, when Papa had come home from town very much excited. "Naomi, I've sold the farm. We'll move over near St. Joseph this fall to be ready to start for Oregon in the spring. I hear more people will be going than went this year."

"I hoped you had given up that idea."

"Only postponed it because Matilda was sick."

"But how do we dare start out with six young children when we don't even know whether a wagon can go through to Oregon?"

"Dr. Whitman says—"

"I hate that Dr. Whitman. I wish you had never heard of him."

Papa put his arms around her. "Naomi, it is for you I want to go. Dr. Whitman said that in Oregon nobody has the chills and fever the way you do every year. Wouldn't you like to feel well?"

"Of course I would, but I wish we could wait until the children are older. What if we have another baby next spring?"

Papa looked surprised. Then he shrugged. "If we do, we won't be the only ones. If people waited around to be through having babies, they'd never get to Oregon. All right, Naomi, I'll admit it is for myself as well as for you that I want to go. I've wanted it for years, and you know it."

"I know you are a Sager, and they all have itchy feet. Your sister told me about it. Your great-grandfather, in Switzerland, felt he had to move to Germany. And your grandfather had to come across the ocean to this country. And your father could not bear to stay in his nice home in Virginia, so he moved to Ohio. And then you had to leave Ohio for Missouri."

Papa grinned while Mama went on, "We've been here five years and have such a good farm. I can't bear to give it up. Who knows what sort of place we'll find out there in Oregon if we live to get there? Somehow, I have a feeling we never will."

"That's not like my stout-hearted Naomi."

"What's stout-hearted, Papa?" Catherine asked.

"It means brave and determined to finish what you begin."

"Are we children stout-hearted?

"Of course. All the Sagers have been stout-hearted or Great-Grandfather would never have gotten to Germany or Grandfather to the United States or my father to Ohio or we here to Missouri. Now we are heading for the Willamette Valley in Oregon. We'll have to be stout-hearted to get there, but we will. Naomi, I promise you this. When we get to Oregon, I'll never ask you to move again."

"Is that a real promise?" Mama asked.

"It is. I'll build you the best house you have ever had."

"Can I have a parlor with no beds in it?"

"You certainly can. And whatever furniture you want, I'll make it for you."

"A hutch cupboard for my new dishes?"

6

Papa looked startled. "What new dishes?"

"The ones I'm going to buy with the money I've earned doing embroidery and sewing for other people these last five years. Why did you think I was doing it?"

"I guess I never noticed you were."

"I have enough for the dishes right now, and I'll need a hutch cupboard to keep them in."

Papa shook his head. "All right, I'll make you a hutch cupboard. And a new table, and a chair for everyone in the family. And bedsteads for all the beds. No more straw ticks on the floor. How about that?" He laughed and tickled her chin.

By this time Mama was laughing too, and Catherine felt better about going to Oregon. Papa had agreed they could take their furniture as far as St. Joseph, but when it came to packing the wagon for Oregon, everything heavy would have to be left behind.

"Except my cherrywood chest," Mama insisted. "Henry, I simply cannot leave that. My mother gave it to me, and she had it from her mother. That is one thing you could not make."

"All right, we'll take that and our two chairs. That is all we'll have room for."

"Except my new dishes, of course."

"We can buy dishes in Oregon."

"How do you know they have stores out there?"

"Naomi, use a little common sense. Dishes are too heavy to take. Besides, they probably would get broken."

Mama had said no more, but every now and then Catherine had seen her counting the money she kept in an old sock, so she knew Mama had not given up about the dishes.

Papa also wanted to leave behind the great sacks of woolen rags Mama had been saving. She never threw away any old clothes. When they could no longer be patched or made over, she put them in a sack saying she would weave a rag rug or carpet some day. "So this winter is when I'll do it," she told Papa. "I'll have a nice new carpet for my new house in Oregon. I'll weave it in a long strip, and we can roll it in canvas to sit on in the wagon."

Right after breakfast on this first morning in the new home Papa and the boys set up the loom, and Mama began to string the warp to make her new carpet. She liked to weave and hummed as she worked. Catherine thought she seemed almost happy about going to Oregon.

Papa was happy, too. He set up his usual blacksmith shop in an open shed near the house, and before long he had plenty of business making wagon tires, plowshares, and horseshoes. It seemed as if everyone was planning to go to Oregon in the spring.

After supper, each evening, Mama gathered the children around the table for an hour of school. She had been a teacher before she married Papa and had a few readers, spellers, and arithmetic books.

"I hope there will be a school in Oregon," she said. "The boys have gone almost as far as I can take them."

"Sure there will be a school," Papa replied. "Must be some teachers among the emigrants. Wouldn't surprise me if there's an academy or college in Oregon some day."

John's eyes shone and Catherine asked, "Could I be a teacher, like Mama?"

"Why not?" Papa was so happy to think they were going that he was ready to hope and believe anything.

As the months passed, the Sager family had such a good time together that Mama said it was the happiest winter they had ever known. Then, all too soon, it was over.

CHAPTER TWO

As early as March, emigrants poured into St. Joseph, and all the talk was of the coming migration. Travelers returning from the West reported that the wagon train of 1843 had safely crossed the Blue Mountains, the hardest part of the journey. Most of the people had gone on down to the Willamette Valley, though some who were sick had spent the winter at the Whitman place on the Walla Walla River. It was lucky the doctor had built it there, just over the Blue Mountains—a good place to buy supplies and rest the oxen. A few persons had died on the plains. This was regrettable, Papa said, but some would have died if they had stayed in Missouri. That was the way of life; some lived and some died. He thought it remarkable that most of the eight hundred men, women, and children had reached Oregon. That fact made Mama hopeful, and John and Frank could hardly contain their excitement.

"How soon can we start, Pa?"

"Not until late April or early May. The grass must be high enough so the oxen can graze."

"Wouldn't it be better to wait until June?" Mama suggested.

"No. We'd be alone, and that is not safe."

With the first signs of spring, Papa dragged their big wagon up near the house, where it would be easy to load, and began preparing it for the journey to Oregon.

By late April everything was ready. Mama's rag carpet, in a big roll, was neatly wrapped in clean canvas. Her new dishes, white china sprinkled with tiny pink rosebuds, were packed in a small barrel with bran from the flour mill around them, so that no two dishes touched. She cried a little when she sold her loom, but Papa said he would make a better one when they got to Oregon.

He kept his promise about taking the cherrywood chest. They had to carry extra clothing somewhere, and he guessed it might as well be there, on top of Mama's linen sheets, pillowcases, and tablecloths. He and the boys had a hard time lifting it into the wagon.

"One thing sure, we won't move it again short of Oregon," he said when they had placed it in the middle to divide the wagon into two parts and had roped it to the sideboards.

In the back space he laid a clean piece of canvas on the floor, then spread on it slabs of bacon and half a dozen hams. Next came the sacks of flour, cornmeal, sugar, beans, dried peas, and a few precious small bags of dried apricots, peaches, pears, and raisins. Last came the mattresses stuffed with straw, the feather beds, quilts, and blankets. The pile almost touched the wagon cover, but somehow there was still room for a box that held Mama's long-handled, three-legged skillet and her Dutch oven.

In the front half Mama and the girls would sleep on the mattresses. Papa and the boys were to have a tent. In one front corner, held by straps, stood the churn, handy for pouring in extra milk night and morning. By the time they stopped again, the motion of the wagon would have made butter for the next meal.

Behind the churn stood the small water cask and, behind that, a bushel basket holding the pewter and tin dishes, eating utensils, and a pile of clean dish towels. At the front on the other side, Papa carefully roped the barrel of dishes. Next to that he laid a bundle of dry firewood for emergencies. The folded tent, laid over the carpet roll, made a comfortable seat for Mama. This left a small space in the middle where the little ones could play safely.

Arched hickory bows, a few feet apart, supported the wagon cover. Papa had fastened hooks to the bows where the family could hang articles that might get lost or be in the way: his gun, slung in loops of cloth, Mama's and the girls' best bonnets, packed in a bandbox, dipper gourds and the little girls' dolls, hung by strings. Pockets in the canvas covering held combs, brushes, and sewing needs. At each end, the canvas could be thrown open for air or closed by drawstrings to small peepholes.

Outside the wagon body, at the front, Papa's toolbox rode on one side, the tent poles on the other. The water bucket and tar bucket hung on a pole beneath. The tailgate could be let down on chains to form a small table where Mama could prepare food. It would also be a dinner table for her and Papa, with the two chairs that were lashed on behind when the wagon was loaded. Mama said a table and chairs would make her feel much more decent and civilized. The children thought it would be fun to eat sitting on the ground, like a picnic. The wagon looked very neat when it was finally loaded.

They came to the last night in the little log house. As they lingered around the supper table, Mama said, "We've been so happy here, all together, I hate—"

"We'll still be all together, Naomi," Papa interrupted. "Isn't that what counts?"

Mama's chin came up. "Of course. Now then, everyone must have a warm, soapy bath. It may be the last for a long time."

Papa brought in the wooden washtub that had to be left behind because it was so heavy. Mama poured in hot water, then cooled it to a comfortable temperature. They all went through the same suds, beginning with Louise and working right along in order of their ages, with Mama coming after the girls, then the boys and Papa.

After the children were in bed, Mama washed out their soiled underclothes in the bath water, rinsed them, and hung them on a line before the fireplace.

Catherine lay awake, too excited to sleep. She heard Mama pad across the floor to her bed. Papa still sat by the fireplace, mending a shoe sole. Her sisters slept beside her, the boys in the loft, all here together, snug and safe. Her throat swelled, and she felt tears on her cheeks. Why should they go away when it was so lovely here? What if something should happen to Mama or Papa on the long journey to Oregon?

She woke to an April morning splashed with sunshine, the sky a clean-swept, heavenly blue, the road dry and smooth. Already, wagons were beginning to pass on their way to St. Joseph.

"Up, everyone," Papa called. Catherine laughed at herself for her worries of the night before. How silly she had been! Nothing was going to happen to spoil their wonderful journey. She pulled on her clean clothes and picked up Louise.

"Come, baby, Sister will dress you. We're going to Oregon."

The morning was half gone before they were ready, but at last everything was done. Papa helped Mama to her seat and then lifted Matilda and Louise in. Catherine and Elizabeth were allowed to run beside the wagon to gather wild flowers; John and Frank walked behind to drive the spare oxen and Bossy, the cow.

"Our friend, Mr. Chamberlain, asked me to stop at his place in St. Joseph," Papa said. "Something there I want you to see, Naomi."

He was so mysterious about it that when he helped Mama down from the wagon, all the children tumbled after, chattering like jaybirds. Catherine clutched Elizabeth's hand as they followed the grown folks into the Chamberlain kitchen and stared in amazement at an object on the far side of the room, a large, square, black iron box mounted on four short legs. A black iron pipe, bigger around than a man's boot, led from the box up to a hole in the ceiling.

"Is that a cookstove?" Mama's voice shook.

"Right the first guess. I knew you would like to see it."

"I've heard of them, but I've never seen one before." Mama walked slowly around the stove, which was set out far enough from the wall so one could pass behind it.

Mrs. Chamberlain, obviously proud of her treasure, showed Mama and the children all its wonderful secrets: a firebox along the front with a small door at the end where one pushed in sticks of wood; four holes for kettles in the top, with lids to fit them; a door at one side opening into an oven.

"Just imagine, Henry! No bending over a fireplace or baking in a skillet. Do you suppose—"

"I knew that would come next. Yes, when we get to Oregon, you shall have a cookstove."

Mama laughed. "Let's hurry."

"Everyone in?" Papa called. "Oregon, here we come."

CHAPTER THREE

All afternoon more and more wagons appeared on the road. Horses, oxen, and mules stirred up a fearful dust. Catherine and Elizabeth, riding in the wagon with Mama and the little ones, could hardly breathe.

"Will it be like this all the way to Oregon?" Mama called to Papa.

"Very likely. We'll get used to it, I guess."

Late in the day he drove off the road to a pleasant spot beside a small stream. He and the boys set up the tent and staked out the animals where they could graze but not get away. Mama spread a cold supper and made coffee over a small fire. Then she said it was time for bed.

Their first night sleeping in the wagon! Elizabeth snuggled close to Catherine and giggled. "Isn't this fun? I think going to Oregon is just wonderful. How long do you think it will take?"

"All summer, Papa said," Catherine replied.

"Oh, goody! I wish it would take forever."

In the morning the sun shone and the birds sang in the trees. During the night the dust had settled, and since they were among the first ones on the road, the air was clear and clean.

"What is that smell?" Catherine asked Papa after they had been driving for a while.

He sniffed. "The smell of the river. The big old Missouri. We're coming near the landing where we cross."

He turned back the wagon cover at the front. Catherine stood behind the high seat. As the road turned, she could see the glint of sunshine on water. Then the river lay before them, gray and misty. "It looks a thousand miles wide. How can we cross it?" she asked.

He pointed with his whip. Far away, Catherine saw something that looked like a small raft floating on the stream. "That's the ferry," he explained.

Mama came up beside Catherine. "It looks terribly dangerous."

"Not if the wagon wheels are properly blocked," Papa replied. "You'll be perfectly safe."

"You will be with us, won't you?" Mama asked worriedly.

"No, I'll have to swim the cattle across. They aren't allowed on the ferry."

"I'll be scared to death just looking at the water."

"Then don't look. Stay inside. You don't need to see the river at all," Papa suggested.

Catherine shuddered. "Papa, let's go back. Let's stay in Missouri."

Papa turned his head. "Catherine, I'm surprised at you. You are a Sager, remember? You can be brave and set a good example to the other girls. Promise me you will."

Catherine drew a deep breath. "I'll try."

"That's my girl."

As they swung around another bend in the road, Mama exclaimed, "Just look at all the wagons and people."

Spread out like the spines of a great fan pointing down to the river were rows and rows of wagons and tents.

"How long will it take all of them to cross?" Mama asked.

"I don't know," Papa replied.

A guide gave him a numbered card. "When your turn comes, your number will be called. There are so many ahead of you, it will be several days," he was told.

"I'm glad we have some time to rest and watch how it goes," Mama said.

Papa swung the wagon into the space allotted to him with the tent beside it. He and the boys led the oxen away to the grazing grounds but kept the cow nearby. Mama insisted that Matilda and Louise stay with her, but Catherine and Elizabeth stood shyly watching other children who were playing games in an open meadow. Soon they were running and shouting like the others. Going to Oregon got better every day, they told each other.

Many families had been accompanied this far by friends and relatives. As parting time, came near, much hugging and kissing went on, shouts of good-bye, many tears and last-minute words of advice. Then, as the ferry moved away and grew smaller in the distance, the weeping friends dragged themselves up the bank to their own horses or wagons. Watching them, Catherine felt a touch of uneasiness. Could it be that going to Oregon was not so much fun as she and Elizabeth thought?

When their own turn approached, Papa hitched Buck and Barney, their strongest team, to the wagon to hold it back as it slid down the incline to the ferryboat, then led them away. Catherine watched through the front peephole as Papa went to a waiting rowboat, tied Jake to the stern, and picked up the oars. The other oxen, one by one, followed Jake. Only Bossy seemed reluctant to get into the water, but John and Frank gave her a push, then ran for the ferryboat.

Mama called to Catherine, "Better lie down so you won't fall if the wagon should lurch."

Shouts, cries, sudden lunges, and they began to move out into the current of the wide Missouri, bobbing up and down like a chip. Louise screamed, and Mama cuddled her close. When Matilda whimpered, Catherine drew her up where she could hide her head in her sister's arms. Catherine's own teeth chattered, but she patted Matilda and murmured, "There, there, honey, it's all right."

It seemed hours before they heard John shout, "Pa's across. I can see him going up the bank leading Jake."

Elizabeth could wait no longer. She scrambled up, steadying herself by grasping the churn, the sideboards, then the high seat until her eyes came up to the peephole. There, just a little way beyond the ferryboat, lay beautiful solid land once more.

Catherine left Matilda on the feather bed and jumped up beside Elizabeth. They saw the workmen let down the gangplank. John untied the rope that held up the wagon tongue. As the wagon rolled off the boat, he and Frank managed to guide it to one side where Papa could hitch on the oxen. There he came now, leading Jake, with all the others trailing behind.

Just then, a little dog appeared from nowhere and began to bark and leap at the legs of one of the oxen. The ox snorted and pawed, but the little beast kept up its barking and jumping. The ox tossed its head, swung around, and started back into the river. In an instant every one of the oxen had plunged in behind. Even Jake tore the rope from Papa's hands and followed the others while the dog continued to bark and leap in a frenzy of excitement. Only Bossy did not run.

Papa started toward the river, then turned back, shaking his head. Catherine knew he was saying, "It's no use." He stood like a person in a dream, staring out across the water.

17

"What's wrong?" Mama demanded. She pulled herself up to look out of the peephole. "Henry, what has happened? Where are the oxen?"

Papa came over to the wagon, his face red and angry looking. "The oxen have gone back to Missouri. That dog! That—"

"Henry, don't swear in front of the children."

Papa took off his hat, brushed back his tousled hair, and put the hat back on. "You know I never swear, Naomi. Now I'll have to go after them. At least, Bossy had sense enough not to run. Tie her up, Frank, before she changes her mind. John, get a few men to help you roll the wagon farther off to the side. Take care of your mother and sisters till I come back. No telling how far I'll have to go."

He leaped to the ferryboat, now ready for the return trip, and was soon out of sight. Mama sank to the floor again and moaned, "Oh, I knew we should never have left our home. I just knew it."

"Someone has to do something," Catherine thought. She lifted Matilda until she could look through the peephole. "See, there's Brother John. He's getting those men to help him. They are going to give us a ride."

As the wagon began to roll, she set Matilda down again, took her doll from its hook, and said, "Hold dolly so she won't be scared." Then she picked up Louise. "Don't cry, baby. In a few minutes John will come to get us."

Mama sat up, wiping her eyes. "I'm sorry I went to pieces. I guess I'm not very brave."

"You are, too. You are the bravest one of all," Catherine said staunchly.

Mama patted her hand. "You are a great comfort to me. If only Papa comes back safely."

"He will. That silly little dog! Oxen are stupid creatures, aren't they?"

"No more stupid than I am." She laughed, and everything was all right again.

John climbed in at the back. "We're all set in a good place, Ma. Frank and I are hungry. Could we have some dinner?"

"Of course. You slice some ham. Katie, cut up those cold potatoes left from breakfast while Frank builds a fire."

The little camp looked very cozy, Catherine thought as she spread a dish towel for a tablecloth. It was a good thing they were near the river since it was the only place with any shade. The new leaves on the cottonwood trees were still small and the lovely green seen only in early spring. In the cool breeze they fluttered like butterflies. The shadows of floating clouds passed over the grass of the prairie like blue ships on a green ocean. Everything was clean and beautiful.

"This would be a nice place to live," she said as they ate.

"I was thinking the same thing," Mama answered. "I wish—" The frightened look came back into her eyes.

Catherine said hastily, "Probably Oregon will be lots prettier."

John set Mama's chair in the shade, where she could sit with her sewing and watch the river. The girls played nearby, and the boys helped people drag their wagons off the ferry every time it came in. One man came up to Mama and told her he had seen her husband on the other side, still chasing the oxen. He had said to tell her he would be gone all night.

Mama did not seem to worry until the third day, when the last of the waiting people had crossed the river and gone on. Then she wrung her hands and cried again. "What are we going to do? How can we ever catch up with the others? I wish we had all gone back to Missouri. The oxen were the only ones with any sense."

Just before dark, the boys called out that they could see a rowboat coming.

The girls rushed down to the river. Sure enough, it was Papa, with a string of oxen behind the boat and beyond them two other men on horseback, swimming their mounts to keep the oxen from turning back.

"I don't know how to thank you," Papa said when all were safely ashore and the troublesome animals hobbled. Now that it was over, he could laugh as he told Mama, "They went all the way back to our log house before I could catch them. Never saw them travel so fast. If they would keep up that pace, we'd be in Oregon in a couple of weeks."

With Papa safely returned, Mama was her old self again. She baked some of her good biscuits, fried ham and potatoes, and opened one of her few glasses of jelly. The friends stayed all night, rolling up in blankets under the wagon. Early in the morning they helped Papa hitch Buck and Barney, Jake and Ike, to the wagon, lifted Mama over the endgate, and boosted in the children.

Papa cracked his long whip, and once more they started for Oregon.

CHAPTER FOUR

Before the day was over, the pleasant weather gave way to rain. In an hour the wagon cover was soaked, and if one touched it, drops of water came through to drip on whatever lay beneath—bedding, clothing, or an upturned face. The canvas was old and mildewed since Papa had bought it years before when the family first moved westward from Ohio. When it was wet, the smell was sickening. The constant jolting of the springless wagon added to the misery.

Catherine was first to be sick to her stomach, but soon all her sisters and then Mama became ill, groaning at each lurch and sway. Papa, sitting out in the fresh air, guessed they had eaten too much breakfast. Mama said riding in the wagon was as bad as a ship. They were seasick.

Papa was so eager to catch up with the rest of the wagon train that he kept going until late at night, then camped in the road. At the first sign of daylight, they started on again. In a few days of hard driving, they reached the place where the roads from Independence and Liberty joined the St. Joseph trail. Here all the wagons had stopped, and the men were holding meetings to organize for the long trip ahead. Altogether, this year of 1844, more than fourteen hundred men, women, and children had come together in two hundred and fifty wagons with several thousand cattle. Obviously they could not all travel as a unit.

Someone suggested they should divide into companies like an army. This seemed a good idea. They elected a general and four captains and drew lots to divide the rest. The Sagers were assigned to the company headed by Captain William Shaw. He and his wife had five boys and one girl and took an interest in all the families in their company. The captain soon knew everyone's name, and Mrs. Shaw had become Aunt Sally to all the children.

Once the train was under way, the men drilled in military style every evening and took turns standing guard through the night. A young man who had brought his drum sounded the calls for duty. Even the children took to drilling. It was all fun and exciting for a week or two. Then, since nothing happened, the men stopped drilling and even neglected to set guards.

One morning, a number of cattle were missing. Captain Shaw studied the tracks in the dust and said Indians had come in the night. Those who had lost cattle leaped onto horses and set out to find them, but it was no use. After this, everyone was alert to the least sound that might mean an attack.

Late one evening when a gunshot crackled, the whole camp burst into an uproar. Papa leaped into the wagon, grabbed his gun, and rushed off into the darkness with John and Frank close behind him. Louise and Matilda began to scream. Catherine and Elizabeth, still feeling weak and sick, peeked under the canvas cover but, dissatisfied with what they could see, crawled out to the wagon seat. All around them in the darkness men were rushing toward the source of the gunshot, crying out the fearful word, "Indians!"

"Catherine! Elizabeth! Come back inside," Mama commanded feebly, but the girls were much too excited to obey.

Suddenly, from far off across the camp ground, came muffled laughter mingled with swear words neither of the Sager girls had ever heard before. Papa appeared out of the darkness, grumbling and laughing at the same time. "Everyone is mad," he told Mama. "A fellow and his girl decided to enjoy a little stroll, and a guard mistook them for Indians. Lucky he was so nervous he missed them or we'd have had a funeral on our hands."

The next morning the captain called a meeting and laid down strict rules about moving around camp after the drum called out the night guards.

One day Mrs. Shaw came to see Mama. When she learned of the persistent "seasickness," she said to Catherine, "You girls must get out and walk in the fresh air, rain or shine. You will soon feel better. Come on, I'll help you out."

Catherine did not want to move, but Mama motioned her to go. She crawled to the back of the wagon, and Aunt Sally helped her to the ground. Elizabeth followed. Holding hands, they tottered along the road, and before long they really did begin to feel better. The next day they took Matilda and Louise out with them. Only Mama said she could not walk. She lay on the feather bed almost all the time.

The weather turned fine again. Everyone said hopefully that now the rains must be over. They settled down to an orderly routine. They broke camp early, after a hearty breakfast, stopped for a cold lunch and a rest at noon, then resumed the march until late afternoon. Some days they made twenty miles, other days no more than ten, depending on the condition of the road and the number of people who were injured or became ill—far too many of both.

In the Shaw company two persons died of camp fever, a strange illness something like typhoid and pneumonia combined. At each death, the whole wagon train stopped while a grave was dug and a brief funeral service held.

In spite of the gloom cast by these unfortunate events, the train moved forward, and people soon recovered their high spirits. On warm evenings fiddles, drums, and mouth organs tuned up, setting young feet to dancing. The evening became a medley of music, whirling calico skirts, snapping fingers, and laughter.

Catherine and Elizabeth were allowed to sit on the wagon tongue for a while and watch, but Papa stayed in the wagon with Mama. Catherine guessed she must be sick, but when she asked Papa, he said, "No, she is only very tired. She will be all right after a while."

Catherine cooked the breakfast mush and sometimes the evening meal as well, her brothers kept the fire going, and Elizabeth unpacked the dishes from the big basket. Afterwards, they washed and dried them together, then repacked them for the next day. Sometimes Mama came out to eat, sometimes not. She hardly paid any attention to them, so they spent little time in the wagon but ran, screamed, played, and fought with the other children, as wild and unrestrained as young animals.

One day, in the middle of the morning, Mama called out to Papa, "You'd better stop, Henry."

He drew the wagon off the road and yelled to John and Frank, who had been walking a little way ahead, to unyoke the oxen and lead them back to the cattle column. Looking scared, they drove the oxen away on the run.

Papa lifted out the two smaller girls, sent Elizabeth to bring Aunt Sally Shaw, and said to Catherine, "Take Matilda and Louise away somewhere."

Catherine stood silent and bewildered. What had happened? Was Mama dying?

Captain Shaw rode along the line, shouting that the train

would stop for the day. Aunt Sally ran up, breathless, followed by Elizabeth, who looked as frightened as Catherine felt. Aunt Sally beckoned to them. "You girls take the little ones over to our wagon. My daughter will give you some dinner. You stay there until I tell you to come back."

All the way to the Shaw wagon, Catherine was aware of women standing in small groups near the halted teams and of children staring at Elizabeth, Matilda, Louise, and her. What was wrong? Did Elizabeth know? She looked sidewise at her sister, but she walked with her head down, eyes on the ground. Catherine wanted to ask someone if Mama was dead, but she did not dare. Obediently, she and her sisters sat down in the shade of the wagon and ate the beans and bacon offered them. Then the Shaw girl went away and left them alone.

The May afternoon was warm and sunny, the prairie bright with wild flowers, pink, blue, and yellow. Catherine led the way to where the flowers were thickest. She and Elizabeth braided them into wreaths for their little sisters, then coaxed them to lie on the grass for naps. For hours the two of them sat silent. Catherine had never felt so lonesome and neglected in all her life. She wanted to talk about it with Elizabeth, but somehow she could not.

The sun was sinking when she heard Aunt Sally calling and ran to her wagon.

"You children have a beautiful little baby sister," she said. "You may go to see her if you are very quiet. Your mama needs rest."

A baby sister! "Another little sister to be dressed and undressed," thought Catherine. She did not want to see the baby, but Aunt Sally stood there waiting, and there was nothing else to do. She started toward their own wagon, the others trailing behind her.

She climbed in and slowly crept along the floor to where Mama lay, smiling weakly. She drew back the blanket from a tiny, red, wrinkled face and said, "Isn't she sweet?"

Catherine thought the baby very ugly, but of course she could not say that to Mama. She whispered, "She's awfully little, isn't she?"

"About the size of all my babies."

"What are you going to name her?" Catherine inquired.

"Papa has a sister named Rosanna. I thought that would be a pretty name for her."

"Hello, Rosanna." She touched the doll-like hand, and the little fingers curled around one of her own. Something seemed to clutch at her heart. "My little sister," she thought and loved her.

"Write it in the Bible that she was born on the thirty-first of May," Mama whispered.

Elizabeth came in next, then Matilda, both staring at the baby but saying nothing. When Louise saw the baby in Mama's arms, she began to scream and kick. If Catherine had not held her hands, she would have struck at the tiny red face.

"Take her out please, Katie. You'll have to sleep in the tent with her and try to keep her quiet. She's jealous, but she will soon get over it."

John carried some of the blankets and a straw tick to the tent and made up a bed for the four girls. He and Frank said they would sleep under the wagon. Mama would need Papa with her.

Matilda, always a peaceable child, snuggled down by Elizabeth and promptly went to sleep, but Louise sobbed and cried and tried to break away from Catherine until she could fight no longer. She subsided in a small heap of misery just inside the tent flap. Too tired to try to move her, Catherine tucked a blanket over her and went to sleep herself.

26

She had no idea what time of night it was when she was roused by the smell of smoke and scorched wool and the sound of a child's voice wailing, "Mama. Mama." Immediately she guessed what had happened. Louise had wakened and started to find Mama, dragging her blanket through the embers of the campfire. Catherine screamed, John and Frank leaped from under the wagon, Papa burst through the open canvas cover, and together they put out the fire.

"It's no use, Naomi. I'll have to sleep in the tent. If you need me, call good and loud."

He lay down across the tent opening, and Catherine once more held the shrieking Louise until she sobbed herself to sleep. Days passed before she would look at the baby without trying to strike her.

CHAPTER FIVE

Captain Shaw held the train in camp for another day to give Mama time to gather strength for more of the bumping and swaying, then they moved on. Rain began again, heavier than before. Everyone said it was the rainiest spring the Missouri Valley had ever known. For almost the whole month of June the travelers rarely saw the sun. Almost everyone had a cold; many were down with strange fevers.

Papa, although half sick himself, went from wagon to wagon prescribing poultices and hot drinks, though seldom was there a chance to heat water. In the steady downpour it was almost impossible to build a fire. Food was poorly cooked if at all. The children, damp and feverish, did not want to eat the half-raw bacon, but Papa insisted. "It will give you strength," he told them. Only Bossy's warm milk tasted good.

Catherine and her sisters cowered in the wagon through terrible storms of thunder and lightning—worse, Mama said, than she had ever known before. Papa and the boys struggled to calm the frightened oxen and keep them moving. No matter what happened in the way of weather, the wagons must go forward, though it might be only a few miles a day.

To pass the long hours, Frank invented a new game, which he taught to Catherine and Elizabeth when the little ones were napping. To play the game, one stepped down from the high seat to the wagon tongue while the vehicle was in motion, then jumped over the flank of the off ox to the ground. The one who jumped farthest and still landed on his feet won the game. Both Catherine and Elizabeth, being light and wiry, were good at it and often beat Frank. Catherine, especially, loved it. Jumping made her feel like a bird, flying.

A neighbor walking past one day said, "Don't you kids know that is dangerous? You might fall and get hurt."

"Pa lets us do it," Frank replied.

Mama, lying in the wagon, called out to know what the man had said and why. She asked Papa, "Do you think it is safe for the girls to jump from the wagon when it is moving?"

"They don't have much fun, Naomi. Long as they are careful, I think it's all right."

At last, on the Fourth of July, the sun came through, the best celebration they could have, Mama said. Since they were the last company in line and their stopping would not hinder the others, Captain Shaw gave them a day of rest so the women could air and dry the damp clothing and bedding. If they could once get dry, Papa said, people would recover from the colds afflicting so many. He and Mama were both coughing.

When the wagons came to the Platte River, everyone enjoyed seeing trees for a few days, but soon they were moving over the prairie. This was buffalo country. Herds of the huge animals covered the plains as far as one could see. Papa had been waiting for this; hunting was his favorite sport. He let John take over the driving while he borrowed a horse and dashed off with the other hunters. He brought back not only buffalo meat but antelope as well. Everyone in camp had so much meat that they did not know what to do with it.

The more experienced ones showed the others how to build scaffolds of sticks and dry thin slices of the meat over small fires. It was then called jerky and would keep for weeks or even months. Frank became expert at feeding the fire just enough to dry but not burn the meat. Even with this way of preserving it, however, a great deal of meat spoiled from being exposed to the hot sun for too long, and Papa said they would be sorry some day for having been so careless and wasteful.

The Shaw company came at last to the ford of the South Fork of the Platte River. The water was shallow but spread out over a great width. A wagon had to keep moving or the wheels would sink in quicksand.

Everything went well for the Sagers until they were pulling up the steep grade beyond the river. The road had been cut from the slope of a hill with an embankment on one side. Something frightened the nervous animals. In spite of Papa's frantic cries and blows, they ran up the bank. Over went the wagon, throwing Mama, the baby, and all four girls to the hard ground. Catherine heard Papa yelling for help.

"Elizabeth," she called.

"I'm all right, Katie, but I can't move."

"Lie still. Papa will come."

Louise began to cry in little gasps as if the breath had been knocked out of her body, but at least she was alive.

Matilda cried out that her arm hurt. So she, too, was alive.

"Mama?" No answer. Catherine saw the cover move at one corner of the wagon, and Papa peeked in.

"I'm here, Papa. I'm all right."

"Thank God for that. Naomi, are you hurt?"

Still no answer. Papa began clawing at the canvas. Catherine could see his face, red and bleeding where the bows had scraped it as the wagon went over. Other men came quickly to help, and they lifted out the children, one at a time.

Catherine's dress had been torn, but she was not badly hurt. Neither were the other children. Only Mama lay still, the baby clutched in her arms.

Papa gently took the little one away and gave her to Catherine to hold. She went to the side of the road, where the wagon wheels had cut in so deeply that they left a bank high enough to sit on. Rosanna lay quiet except for an occasional sob that shook her whole body.

Catherine cuddled her and spoke softly to her. Never, she thought, had she loved anyone as she loved this helpless. "If Mama is dead, I'll take care of you as long as I live," she promised.

"Put up the tent," Papa called to John and Frank, who had come running when someone told them their wagon had tipped over.

They dug the tent from the wreckage and set it up nearby. Papa and another man carefully lifted Mama and carried her inside. Louise began to scream when she caught sight of Mama lying so still. John swung Louise to his shoulders and jogged up and down the road. She stopped her crying and kicked him with her little bare heels. "Giddap, horsie. Go faster."

"He always seems to know what to do with her," Catherine said to herself.

Matilda ran to Frank, "Ride me, ride me."

"You're too heavy. Let's walk together."

Elizabeth sat down beside Catherine. She was still shaking, and Catherine shifted the baby to one arm so that she could put the other around her troubled sister.

"Mama's dead, isn't she?" Elizabeth whispered.

"We don't know."

31

Many men had come. They righted the wagon, untangled the frenzied oxen, and rehitched them. Under Frank's direction they began repacking the wagon. It seemed a miracle that not much was broken, only thrown into a sickening mess, with sour milk from the churn running over everything. Women brought cloths and pans of water; they scrubbed, shook blankets, straw ticks, and feather beds, and put everything back in place.

After what seemed hours, Papa came out of the tent, mopping his forehead. He smiled at the girls. Catherine thought that smile was like the sun breaking through clouds. "She was badly shaken and hurt some, but she will be all right. She wants you to bring her the baby."

Catherine felt as if she had been holding her breath for hours. Now she could let it out. "Mama is alive," she thought, and the wonder of it filled her soul.

Captain Shaw rode up to Papa. "Do you think she can travel?"

"If we must, Captain."

"Even at best it will be dark by the time we get to the camping place the scouts have found."

"All right. Will someone lend me a hand to carry her?"

The boys had the tent down almost before they got Mama out of it. She smiled at the girls. "Oh, but she is a stout-hearted woman," Catherine thought.

Papa saw that everyone was back in the wagon, then climbed to the high seat and cracked his whip. No matter what happened, the wagon train must go on.

CHAPTER SIX

Slowly the travelers moved westward. The rain ceased. In its place came hot July sunshine and dust pouring endlessly up through the cracks in the wagon bed. The prairies were still green, though every day Mama said she could see more brown in the grass. Papa said that was a sign it was curing, like meat over a fire. The cattle seemed to do well on it.

Mama gained strength every day. Often she sat with Papa on the wagon seat, the baby in her arms, while Matilda and Louise played together just behind her in the space where the beds lay at night. Matilda's knee hurt if she walked much, and Louise was such a wild little thing that Mama would not let either of them out of her sight for long.

Catherine and Elizabeth were free most of the time to run along beside the wagon or play with other children. Mama started them out every morning with sunbonnets tied firmly under their chins, but before long the bonnets hung down their backs and their hair came unbraided. Their faces grew tanned, their dresses torn and dirty. Mama said what would people think of her, letting her children run wild? Papa said that did not matter; they were healthy and strong as never before. Often he pointed out to Mama that with all her troubles, she had not had malaria this summer. The West was already curing her.

John and Frank, too, ran wild. Their duty was mainly to help herd the cattle behind the column of wagons. They showed up at mealtimes, dirty and hungry, Frank's eyes dancing at his latest practical joke, John, as always, more steady and reliable but ready to fight for his brother if need be.

Often Papa was called to prescribe for some sick person. Catherine saw him smile as he went from tent to tent with his little bag of medicines. This was what he liked best to do. He even pulled teeth now and then, using a pair of pliers or a turnscrew.

"The last day of July," he announced one night after supper. "I wish these long days would last until we get to Oregon. Just look at that sunset. How bright the colors are here on the prairie!"

Catherine had not thought about that before, but it was true. The dust had settled, so the air was clear; the sunset stretched all the way around to the north like a great pink veil flung over the sky. In the morning, everyone was shivering.

"First day of August. Fall is coming," Papa said. "The captain tells me we should get to Fort Laramie by night."

"What is a fort?" Elizabeth asked.

"A place where people can go for protection. There are high walls around it so no one can get in once the gates are closed."

"Will there be Indians near?"

"I suppose so, but they won't hurt us."

"I'll be glad to see buildings again," Mama said. "Will we stop a few days?"

"The captain says not. We have had so many delays, we are way behind schedule. If we don't move right along, we could get caught by a snowstorm in the Blue Mountains."

At noon the wagon train stopped in a beautiful grove beside the North Platte River. The men and boys took a quick swim; Mama rinsed out the baby's diapers as she did whenever they stopped near a stream.

After an hour's rest, Captain Shaw ordered the train to move on. They left the river and started over a level, sandy plain. The afternoon grew very warm. It seemed impossible that anyone had felt cold at night. Mama urged the girls to rest for a while with her, and all of them went to sleep except Catherine. She lay awake wishing she could get out of the dust boiling up through the floor cracks. Moving silently, she crawled to the front and out to the seat.

Papa was walking beside the oxen, as he often did. Catherine thought she would like to walk with him. She stepped down to the wagon tongue and jumped as she had done dozens of times. She had not noticed that Papa's ax had not been pushed clear into the toolbox at the side and the handle stuck out. As she jumped, her dress caught on it. Down she went, just behind the hoofs of the off ox. She screamed, then everything went black as the heavy wheels passed over her body.

The next thing she knew, she was lying in the road behind the wagon. Papa was kneeling beside her and Mama looking down at her, tears running down her face.

"Catherine, baby! Naomi, she is still alive."

"Of course I am," Catherine tried to sit up, then fell back, the blackness sweeping over her again.

Papa lifted her in his arms, staring at her oddly dangling left leg. "Oh, my dear child, your leg is broken!"

Men came running and put up the tent. Papa carried her inside and laid her on a hastily spread blanket.

"There is a doctor in the next company. I'll get him," she heard a man say.

"Papa, you fix my leg," she whispered.

He did not reply, but gently began straightening her leg. Catherine screamed with the sudden terrible pain.

John and Frank rushed into the tent, panting. "What's happened now?"

"John, bring me some of those thin strips of wood inside the wagon," Papa ordered. "Naomi, I'll need bandages. Bring a sheet from your chest."

It was a bad time for Catherine before the leg lay bandaged in splints to keep it straight, but both Papa and Mama praised her for her bravery. The work had just been finished when they heard the pounding of hoofs and two men burst into the tent.

"This is Dr. Dagon," said their neighbor, who had ridden to bring him.

Catherine looked up into a face almost covered by a bushy beard. Two bright blue eyes looked down at her with a kindness she could feel. The doctor knelt beside her and ran his fingers lightly along her bandaged leg.

"Just as good as I could do mine own self," he said in a thick German accent.

Elizabeth and Matilda, who had crept into the tent behind him, began to giggle at his strange way of speaking, and Mama hustled them outside. Papa and the doctor talked in low tones; then Papa went away for a while and came back carrying a long, narrow box.

"Now then, Catherine, I've made something to carry your leg in till it's well," he said cheerfully. "Mama has padded the inside, and we'll lay your leg in it so the jolting won't hurt so much. Dr. Dagon, let's see if we can get her into the wagon. We've moved things around so there is more room for beds."

Someone brought a canvas stretcher and slid it under Catherine's small body as Papa lifted her. They carried her to the wagon and placed her in a space they had cleared at the other end from Mama's bed.

"That feels better," she whispered, trying to smile as Papa slipped the padded box under her leg.

"Henry, we don't have to go on today, do we?" Mama begged.

"I'll ask Captain Shaw."

When he returned, Catherine heard him talking to Mama outside the wagon. "I'm sorry, Naomi. We have only a few hours of travel to reach Fort Laramie. The captain says we must go on." He was seized with a fit of coughing.

"Your cold is worse."

"Don't bother about me. I'll be all right. But our poor child—if only I had not let them jump over the wheel! I hope I set the leg right. If I didn't, she may never walk again."

"Hush, Henry."

Catherine lay thinking. "Never walk again? Never run and jump again? Oh no, it can't be. I'll keep quiet. I won't cry or make a fuss. Surely it will get well. But oh, if only I had noticed that ax handle!"

During the short stay at Fort Laramie, Elizabeth looked around, then came to report to Catherine. "Just as Papa said. A high log wall with a gate in it. Lots of Indians. They don't look mean."

Dr. Dagon said he would go along with the Sagers for a while to keep watch on Catherine's leg. He did not have a wagon of his own but had been paying for space in another, so it was very little trouble for him to bring his small bag of clothing and medicines and share the tent at night.

"I am very grateful to you," Mama said. "My husband is not well, and the boys also seem to be taking cold."

Papa protested that he was not sick, but one day he could not get up. The boys, too, were obviously very ill. Dr. Dagon examined them, then said soberly, "They all have camp fever. They must stay in bed."

He and Mama moved the piles of bedding and clothing and the dwindling sacks of supplies, making the wagon a moving hospital. Every inch of space was taken by beds. With Dr. Dagon working night and day with poultices and hot drinks, the sick man and the two boys gradually began to recover.

For some time the whole wagon train had been short of supplies, especially meat, and many people wished they had not wasted so much back in buffalo country. It seemed almost unbelievable then when suddenly, one afternoon, a few of the huge animals came galloping clumsily over the prairie. Papa heard the shouts of "Buffalo!" and sprang from his bed.

"Henry, you must not go. You aren't strong enough," Mama protested.

Dr. Dagon shouted in German something Catherine knew must be the same warning. Papa only said, "We need meat," grabbed his gun, and jumped from the wagon.

Hours later he dragged himself back, exhausted and dripping with sweat. Before long he was burning with fever, and Catherine, lying next to him, knew he was terribly sick again.

The doctor did all he could, but this time his remedies did not help. Every day Papa grew weaker until Catherine thought she could not stand to hear him groan and feel his body shake with chills. Finally, out of his mind with fever, he began raving about his farm in Missouri.

One evening after the train had made camp, Captain Shaw came. "How are you feeling, Mr. Sager?"

"I am dying."

"Don't say that, man. You'll pull through."

Papa's voice was very weak. "Captain Shaw, I have heard about that missionary, Dr. Marcus Whitman, and how people can stay at his place over the winter if they need to. Will you take my wife and children there? Naomi is still weak, and this little one here will be a cripple for a long time."

"Of course I will, Mr. Sager, if you aren't up and around by the time we get there, but don't give up hope."

Throughout the night after Captain Shaw's visit, Mama sat by Papa's side, keeping cool cloths on his forehead, but his fever ran so high that Catherine could feel the heat of it through the blankets. Toward morning, she fell asleep, and when she awakened, Mama was pulling a sheet over Papa's face.

"Is he better, Mama?"

Mama had a wild look in her eyes. She hardly seemed to know what she was saying. "Oh, Henry, if only we had stayed in Missouri."

They had camped that night on the banks of the Green River, "a beautiful place," Elizabeth told Catherine. Captain Shaw ordered some of the men to cut down one of the cottonwood trees along the bank. They split it and hollowed out the pieces to make a coffin for Papa, and a minister traveling with them read the funeral service. Catherine could hear most of it from her bed.

"Don't cry, Katie," said Elizabeth, who had stayed with her. "Papa would like to be in such a lovely place, under the trees."

"I wish I could see it," Catherine replied. "Write it in the Bible that he died on the twenty-eighth of August."

After Elizabeth had gone, she could no longer keep from crying. "Oh, Papa, Papa," she sobbed. Then it seemed as if he spoke to her: "Be brave; set a good example for the others." She did not want to be brave, but she had promised, so she wiped her eyes. When Mama came into the wagon and lay down beside her, she whispered, "We'll make it, Mama. We'll get to Oregon as Papa wanted. I'm getting better. I'll soon be up to help you.

"Oh, Katie, what would I do without you?"

CHAPTER SEVEN

People said Mama was wonderful the way she took hold, but soon anyone could see the Sagers were in trouble. Mama was not strong enough to drive, the doctor was not good at it, Frank was too small and light, and John had to take his turn herding the cattle column. Mama said she would have to hire a man who knew how to handle oxen.

That very day a young man came along on horseback, said he had heard she needed help, and asked for the job. Catherine guessed that Dr. Dagon was hurt when he had to give up his place, but he said nothing. For a day or two everything went better.

There had been so many delays for this section of the wagon train that they were again running low on food. When they came to a small trading post called Fort Bridger and found a stream swarming with fish, the company stopped a day. The men used wagon sheets for nets and hauled in great catches of fish that they split and smoked as they had smoked the buffalo meat earlier. This time, they reminded one another, they would not be wasteful.

The new driver told Mama if she would let him take Papa's gun, he would go get a deer. Venison would be a good change from fish, so without consulting John or the doctor, Mama let him have the gun. That was the last they ever saw of the man. When she realized he was not coming back, Mama was so discouraged that she seemed to lose heart.

"Dr. Dagon, I know I shouldn't ask it, but will you drive again?"

"Ach, ya, that I will, so good as I can."

"I have made up my mind that when we get to Fort Hall, I'll trade our wagon and stock for horses. We'll go the rest of the way on horseback as other travelers have done. When we get to the Whitman Mission, we'll stay there all winter."

"But, Ma," John protested, "It's five hundred miles from Fort Hall to the mission. You couldn't ride horseback that far."

"I'll have to try. The jolting of the wagon is killing me. All I want is to get to Dr. Whitman's place as soon as possible."

"You said you hated him," Elizabeth reminded her.

Mama sighed. "I should not have said that, though if it had not been for him, perhaps your dear father would not have decided to take this journey. I don't know. Whatever I said, Dr. Whitman is our only hope. Once there, perhaps I'll get well."

The travelers continued on through the Rocky Mountains. Days were hot but nights and mornings bitterly cold. Mama insisted that Dr. Dagon and the boys take more of the blankets. She and the girls huddled closer together, next to Catherine. A dozen times in the night, Catherine heard her crawling around, pulling up blankets and quilts.

Sometimes she reached out to squeeze Mama's hand, to let her know how brave she was. "Stout-hearted," Papa had called her, but even the stoutest heart failed sometimes. Mama began to cough the way Papa had done. Catherine felt chills race up her own back. Unspoken prayers rose from her heart.

She could sit up now if there was a comfortable place for her, but Dr. Dagon said it would be better for her to stay flat, with her leg in the padded box, while the wagon was moving. In the evening he carried her out to a chair beside the fire. Elizabeth helped her wash and comb her hair. Mama said she was a real helper with the younger children, too.

On the first day of September they reached Fort Hall, a strong fort with high walls of logs and blockhouses at diagonal corners. Indians camped outside in tepees. Some of the travelers wanted to stop here for a rest, but Captain Shaw said they must not waste even one day. By this date they should have reached the Whitman Mission, five hundred difficult miles ahead. Mama said nothing about changing to horses; she was too sick to think of anything.

As they pulled out of Fort Hall, everyone knew they were coming to the most dangerous part of the journey. The trail followed the Snake River. They could see the water for which they longed, but the stream was so deep down in its canyon that no one could get to it. What water they had must be carried from one small creek to another.

The dust was so terrible for Mama that Dr. Dagon hung a sheet at the front, closing the peephole. It kept out a little of the dust, but inside the wagon the air was suffocating. Matilda and Louise made so much fuss that the doctor let them ride up with him, Elizabeth beside them to keep them from falling, while Catherine lay alone with Mama, holding her hand. It was all she could do for her.

At last Mama became so weak that she could no longer nurse the baby. Dr. Dagon went from wagon to wagon, begging the women who had babies to give Rosanna a little of their milk when their own babies did not need it all. She was passed from one to another, each taking a turn. Catherine thought of her every day, but she seldom saw her.

One or other of the kindly neighbors came in every morning and night to wash Mama's face and hands and try to make her more comfortable. Sometimes they brought food for the family—a piece of boiled meat or johnnycake baked in a skillet. Otherwise they ate jerky and mush cooked by the doctor or the boys. Mama could eat nothing.

No longer was there singing and dancing in camp at night; everyone was too tired. Life had become a battle of grim endurance against time, weather, and weakness.

One day Mama roused enough to ask Elizabeth to bring in the rest of the children so she could see them once more. She reached a thin hand to each one.

"John, Frank, promise me you will look after your sisters and try to keep the family together."

Catherine saw the boys wink back tears. "Yes, Mama, we will."

"Be kind to them," Mama murmured and closed her eyes.

Louise wanted to stay with Mama, but John took her away. Frank lifted Matilda out and gave a hand to Elizabeth.

Around the wagon, everything became very quiet. Catherine heard the boys set up the tent. She closed her eyes when the doctor and John carried Mama from her bed. A few minutes later, she felt a hand touch her.

"Did your mother have a nice light-colored dress?" a tearful voice asked.

"Yes, a real pretty one, but I don't know where it is."

Elizabeth climbed in and helped hunt for it, but everything was in such a tangle that they could not find it. They would have to bury Mama in a dark blue calico that needed washing. The doctor lifted Catherine out so that she could watch him and the boys prepare the grave. In this place called Pilgrim Springs, there was no tree large enough to make a coffin like Papa's. They laid willow brush in the bottom of the grave, wrapped Mama's body in a sheet and lowered it, and then spread more brush over it before they filled the grave. It seemed a terrible way for a brave life to end.

John cut a piece of board to place at the head of the grave and lettered Mama's name on it with a charred stick: "Naomi Carney Sager, age 37." Papa was thirty-eight, Catherine remembered; they died only twenty-six days apart.

That night Catherine overheard some of the men talking with Captain Shaw and Dr. Dagon about her, her brothers and sisters. One suggested that they be divided among the other members of the train. Almost any family could take one more child. Captain Shaw said no—he had promised Henry Sager to see his family through to the Whitman Mission. Nobody was going to break up that family while he had anything to say about it.

When Catherine had a chance, she told John what she had heard. He seemed to have grown taller in the last few days; his face was thin, and he looked like a man, not a boy. He took both her hands in his. "Frank and I promised Ma to take care of you girls and keep us all together, and we're going to do it."

Captain Shaw told the boys to bring their wagon up next to his so that he and Aunt Sally could help look after the little ones. Aunt Sally put her arms around Matilda and Louise. "As long as Uncle Billy and I have a loaf of bread, you won't go hungry."

Not only the Shaws took on the responsibility of the Sager family; everyone in the wagon train offered help. Never were children more tenderly cared for, considering the destitute condition in which everyone was living. The children rarely saw their baby sister, but Aunt Sally told them she was still alive. "Mrs. Perkins has her today; tomorrow is Mrs. Eads's turn. They are doing the best they can for her."

The day came when Dr. Dagon removed the splints from Catherine's leg, which looked thin and shrunken but was as straight as the other. "Your papa did a good job," he said. Now, when they camped, Catherine could hobble around a bit, leaning on a forked stick padded to make a crutch. John acted like a father, making Matilda and Louise mind even better than Papa had done. None of the children could speak of their parents, but somehow life began to pick up again.

Everyone, including Captain Shaw, was becoming anxious over the delays they had suffered. Other companies had gone ahead and must already have arrived at the Whitman Mission or gone on down the Columbia River to the Willamette Valley. The Shaw party still had to cross the Snake River and then the much-feared Blue Mountains.

One morning Catherine saw Dr. Dagon and Captain Shaw studying the Sagers' oxen. One had died; the others were very weak. "If we cut down the wagon, the way some of the others are going to do, they might be able to pull it over the mountains," the captain said. "Dr. Whitman had to do the same with his wagon the first time he came across. Must have been just about here that he did it."

The cavalcade had stopped for a day, and everywhere one heard the sounds of hammer and saw. Catherine wanted to cry when she saw the men cut off the back half of their lovely big wagon, of which Papa had been so proud.

"What will we do with all our things?" she asked Aunt Sally.

"We'll have to leave behind everything you do not absolutely need. I know it hurts, but that is what we'll have to do if we are going to get you children across the mountains."

"Mama's cherrywood chest?"

Aunt Sally nodded.

"Her rag carpet and new dishes?"

"Life is more important than things, dearie. If your mama were here, she would be brave enough to do what has to be done. You must do the same."

Catherine helped as much as she could, sitting near the pile of things the doctor took out of the wagon. She emptied the chest of the remaining clothing, sheets, and tablecloths that Aunt Sally said they needed to keep. She and Elizabeth watched the boys set the empty chest beside the road, then the lovely rag carpet and the barrel of dishes. They cried together, remembering how hard Mama had worked to get the money for the dishes and how she had spent all winter weaving the beautiful carpet. Aunt Sally rescued their Bible, saying, "You better keep this. It has your names and ages written in it." Catherine laid the doctor book beside it. "We might need this someday, too."

The wagon had now become a two-wheeled cart. The doctor said they might need the other two wheels before they got through the mountains, so he and the boys lashed them to the cart, one on each side.

"All right, here we go," he said briskly. Catherine knew he felt as bad as the rest of them but was trying to keep up their spirits. She blinked back her tears and with his help climbed into the cart. Elizabeth came next, and the doctor lifted in Matilda and Louise. Last of all, he climbed in himself, but he was too heavy. The front of the cart tipped up, the back went down; doctor, girls, bedding, blankets, and everything else slid to the ground in a pile. John and Frank took time to see that no one was hurt, then they burst into laughter. One by one, the girls scrambled out, and they too laughed at the doctor's sheepish look. It seemed good to laugh again.

CHAPTER EIGHT

Through broiling days and chilling nights, the wagon train struggled along the Snake River: one week, two weeks, three weeks. Several small streams came in from the south, gouging deep cuts in the earth, and to ford them, the wagons had to lurch down one side and crawl up the other. Everyone who could had to walk. Oxen lay down and died; people almost wished they could do the same.

Clothing grew soiled and torn, for there was no water for washing or time in which to do it. Shoes wore out, and no one repaired them. "Papa would have," Catherine told herself. He had always kept their shoes mended and soled and buttons sewed on, but now the girls were barefoot.

The days were bad enough, but the nights were awful. Louise cried herself to sleep, calling for Mama; Matilda made no sound, but tears ran down her face, hurting Catherine more than Louise's cries. She and Elizabeth lay holding each other's hands, trying not to cry but with an awful ache in the throat.

Everyone was hungry. The small remaining stocks of food had to be rationed carefully, but whatever there was, the Sager children received their share. Dr. Dagon ate very little, insisting he was too fat and needed to thin himself down. Bossy the cow, whose milk had kept the two smallest girls going, now gave almost none.

At last came the day when through a gap in the cliffs the travelers saw the trail winding down to the Snake River at the famed Three Islands crossing, one of the few places where wagons could ford the great stream. Here the river spread out a thousand feet wide, but a peculiarity of the current had washed sand into a sort of reef with three humps rising above the water level at this time of year. Between these islands, the sand lay in a path drivers could follow if they were clever and lucky. This was the most dangerous and most feared river crossing on the Oregon Trail. Many stories were told of wagons going down with animals tangled in their harness and of men drowning in an attempt to free them.

While the Sagers waited their turn at the top of the grade, John nailed up the endgate so the girls could not slide out if the cart tipped. As they began the descent, the old cart's wobbly wheels swayed from side to side on the steep, slippery trail, and Catherine could hear John yelling and Dr. Dagon swearing in German at the poor oxen. Matilda and Louise shook with terror in her arms. Catherine was glad they could not see the river; she heard enough from the men's shouts to know it was frightening even to them.

She heard them fasten another wagon beside their cart and remembered that John had told her this was one way of presenting a stronger resistance to the powerful current that might sweep a single vehicle right off the narrow ford into the deep water. A sickening sidewise slip sent the cart into the river, but soon it steadied. Catherine could feel the tug of the current and the pull of the sand on the wheels. Water came up through the cracks in the floor, though John had caulked them with tar. "Pull your feet up into my lap," she told Louise as she felt the ice-cold water curl around her own bare toes. "We're all right; Brother John is out there keeping the oxen on

49

the ford." She tried to sound sure, but inwardly she shook as much as her little sisters. Elizabeth was shaking, too, but she did not say a word.

Suddenly the water drained away; the wheels moved more freely. "We're on the first island," Catherine said, and felt Louise relax a bit. But then came the heart-stopping slide again, the pull of the current, the water around her feet. She remembered that first time they had crossed a stream, the Missouri, and how frightened Mama had been, even though the wagon had rested solidly on the raft and strong men had pulled the sweeps. She was almost glad Mama was not here.

After they crossed the third island, the ford turned upstream, and the oxen almost refused to breast the current. Dr. Dagon swore louder than ever, the whip crackled, and John and Frank yelled, "Get up there, you lazy, good-for-nothings! You can't turn back here." She could hear the thud of sticks on the oxen's flanks and shuddered at what her brothers were doing. They were not mean boys, and she knew they did not like to beat the poor, tired animals. Just then she felt the wagon wheels hit the dry ground; all four girls were pitched backward as the oxen labored up the steep slope. They had safely crossed the Snake.

Captain Shaw headed north toward Fort Boise. Dr. Dagon, who knew a little French, told the children the name Boise came from the French word *bois*, meaning trees or woods. A pleasant thought! Maybe they would once more see trees. At present, however, their trail led over dry, sandy plains and rolling hills where nothing but sagebrush grew. The staggering oxen found little to eat and less to drink, and even babies suffered from thirst. One night the train had to make a dry camp with only the tiniest sips of water for everyone, water they had carried from the Snake.

At Fort Boise there were no trees in sight and little possibility of replenishing the wagon train's supplies. This post out in the desert did not have much to spare, and they were able to buy only a little jerked meat. The children had become so weak and tired that they slept most of the day. Aunt Sally Shaw baked the last of her flour into one loaf of bread and divided it among her own half-starved children and the Sagers. There would be nothing but meat and not much of that until they reached the Whitman Mission.

Soon the steady meat diet made everyone sick. Aunt Sally, feeling miserable herself, came every night to see how the Sager children fared. From somewhere she got a little milk, which she portioned out, saving a few swallows for Dr. Dagon, who was very ill. He said later that the milk saved his life.

"We must somehow get another cow or these children will die before we can cross the mountains," Aunt Sally told her husband.

Not long afterward, she came to the Sager cart leading a poor, broken-down cow whose ribs showed plainly under the skin. "She's not much for looks, but she still gives a little milk," she told the doctor.

"Where did you get her?"

"Billy"—she never called her husband "the captain" as others did—" bought her from an Indian."

"For how much?" He reached for his purse.

Aunt Sally tossed her head. "What matter? Just some old clothes we didn't need. Five dollars' worth at most. Forget it." She drew Louise into her arms. "How would you like a drink of milk, honey?" Then, to the doctor, "If only we can keep them alive till we get to the Whitman Mission."

While the days were still comfortably warm, the nights were freezing cold. The first thing families did when they made camp was to build a fire. Everyone gathered around close, but one night Elizabeth overdid it and her full calico skirt, blown by the wind, swept into the flames. She screamed, and Dr. Dagon leaped to beat out the fire with his bare hands. She was not hurt, but his hands were so badly burned that he could not help with the driving for days.

The next one to cause trouble was Louise. She still cried for Mama at night, and Catherine held her in her arms and sang to her as Mama used to do. Once she had collapsed into sleep, however, Catherine felt sure she would not move until morning, so she let herself relax. Then one night Louise uncovered herself, grew cold, and woke in the darkness. She had moved away from Catherine, and as she felt around the bed, found herself alone.

"Mama," she said softly, then, more loudly, "Mama, Mama."

No one heard her weak little voice. She began to crawl toward the back of the cart. Somewhere out there Mama must be waiting for her. She pulled up her little flannel nightgown, crawled over the endgate, and dropped to the ground.

"Mama," she cried, more loudly now, but still no one answered her. Tripping over the long gown, she began to run. More and more wildly she called, "Mama, Mama," then broke into a prolonged wail.

Sunk deep in sleep, neither Catherine in the cart nor the boys and Dr. Dagon in the tent heard her. But over in the Shaw wagon Aunt Sally roused. What child could be out there in the freezing night, sobbing and crying? She shook her husband's shoulders. "Billy! There's a lost child somewhere outside. Hear it cry?"

The captain stirred and swore under his breath. "Whoever has let their young'un get loose better find it themselves."

"But, Billy, a child could die of cold out there," his wife argued.

Reluctantly the captain crawled out of his warm blankets and went out into the bitter night. The baby voice seemed farther away now, but he could hear the cry, "Mama, Mama, where is you?"

Now he knew who it was—that Sager baby! But how had she managed to get out of the cart? A few minutes' run and he caught up with her and took her up in his big warm arms.

"What are you doing out here, Louise?"

"I went to find Mama."

He carried her to the tent, stooped to get inside, and kicked at the first sleeping form he came to. It happened to be John. "Better watch your little sister closer," he advised as he passed Louise down to the waiting arms. She snuggled down and soon slept again.

CHAPTER NINE

Indians appeared, the first the travelers had seen for some time. The children were afraid of them until Captain Shaw said these called themselves "Doctor Whitman's Indians" and seemed friendly. One of them even came leading an ox that had been left behind but had recovered enough strength to go on. The Indians had learned to raise potatoes and were willing to trade them for guns or clothing. Some men took the shirts off their backs to buy three or four potatoes, so starved were they for starchy food.

The Sagers' cart was so much lighter than the other wagons that they often got ahead of the train, and Dr. Dagon would stop to let the others catch up. No one wanted to be alone for very long. One day while they waited at the top of a hill, freezing in the bitter wind, the doctor suggested they go down beside the creek, out of the wind, and have a cup of tea to warm themselves. Tea was one of the few supplies they had left.

Rain had fallen in the night, and the wood that Frank and Elizabeth gathered was so wet that it would not catch fire. Thinking he would help along a tiny wisp of smoke, Frank upended his powder horn over the pile of wood. Instantly the horn exploded in his hands and knocked him sprawling. He jumped to his feet, dashed to the stream, and plunged his head into the cold water. "Are my eyes red?" he asked the anxious doctor who had run after him.

John and the girls waited while the doctor examined Frank's eyes, then reassured by his verdict of no serious damage, they burst into laughter at the sight of their brother with his face black and his eyebrows and lashes burned off. It was one of the few things they found to laugh at during these harrowing days.

Slowly the company made its way along the Burnt River, over a divide to the Powder River, then into the beautiful Grand Ronde Valley, where there was plenty of grass and a fine, clear stream. It would have been a good place to rest for a few days, but it was now near the end of October. Snow would come soon in the Blue Mountains, looming just ahead.

The mountain crossing took three days. Captain Shaw tried to encourage the men by telling them that the emigration of the previous year had suffered a much worse time when forty men had worked five days to cut a rough trail the wagons could follow. Still, this was not much comfort to men who had to double their teams to pull the wagons up each steep slope, chain the wheels and tie logs on behind to hold them to the grade going down. The last day they woke up to snow, falling gently through the pine forest.

Toward evening the wagons reached an opening in the park-like pine forest where the people could see spread below the great valley of the Columbia River.

"Three hundred miles yet to go along that river before we reach the Willamette Valley," said Captain Shaw.

John, standing near, mused, "That's where Pa wanted to take us."

"So that's where we'll go," Frank said firmly.

Catherine shifted her weight from her aching leg to her crutch. "I thought we were going to the Whitman Mission."

"That's only a perhaps. What if they don't want us?"

The question stayed in Catherine's mind all the next day as the cart slid and rolled down what must surely have been the longest hill in the world. When they reached the Umatilla River, part of the travelers made camp, to rest and repair their wagons and to replenish their food stocks from the potatoes and flour offered for sale by a man Dr. Whitman had sent to the Umatilla camp.

Some of the immigrants complained about paying, thinking the doctor should give them these supplies free. After all, he was a missionary, wasn't he? "But he has to buy seed and pay men to help him," Aunt Sally said. She bought as much as she could pay for, and the family had its first taste of bread in weeks. The potatoes were almost as good.

The Shaw company had come over the Blue Mountains by a different route from that used by the Whitmans eight years before, and to get to their station, it was necessary to turn back eastward about forty miles. Only those who were ill or desperately in need of more supplies than were available here made that extra journey. All who could went on toward the Columbia and the trail westward to The Dalles. There, at the foot of the Cascade Mountains, they would have to build or buy rafts to carry them down the river to Vancouver and the valley. Already, when anyone said "the valley," he meant the Willamette Valley.

Captain Shaw left his family camped with the Sager children while he rode horseback to ask if the missionaries would take the orphaned family. After he left, Aunt Sally helped Catherine wash out a dress for each girl, and John borrowed her dull shears to cut off their tangled, matted hair.

Uncle Billy—as they all called the captain now—rode back into camp late the second day, after the girls had gone to bed in the cart and the boys in the tent. Catherine heard the crackle of flames and the sputter of grease in a pan as Aunt Sally cooked his supper.

"How did you come out?" she asked in a low voice.

"They had already heard about the Sager children. Wagons have been coming in for a month."

"Will they take the children?"

"At first they said no. But they are very religious people. Mrs. Whitman finally sort of left it to the Lord, I guess. If He sends them to her, she will have to take them. That is, if no one else can or will. I told her how it is with us. Anyhow, I don't believe that old cart would hang together long enough to get to the valley. And the children are too weak, specially the two little ones."

"She said she would take the girls for the winter."

"Not the boys? Oh, no, she can't mean to separate them after their parents begged that they might be kept together."

"We must not judge her, Sally. She's been sick a lot, her husband told me. And anyone can see she's got too much to do right now. People running in and out all the time, enough to drive a person crazy. Children all over the place."

"Are they hers?"

"I don't know. Never asked. Some of them looked like half-breeds. Sally, I feel sick about this. If I just knew where we were going to live—how I am going to feed my own family—"

"I know. Why, if we had a house, Billy, like the Whitmans, I'd never let these children go. But we can only do what we can. When will you take the girls over there?"

"We'll start tomorrow morning."

"Let the boys go along. Once she sees them, maybe she will change her mind."

"She doesn't strike me as the kind that changes her mind. But anyhow, let the boys stay with them as long as possible."

Catherine lay still, hardly breathing. Had John and Frank heard? How could she and her sisters live without them? "I don't like Mrs. Whitman," she told herself, "I don't care if she is a missionary, I don't like her."

In the morning, when Aunt Sally was cooking their breakfast of boiled potatoes, Catherine asked, "Do you know where Rosanna is?"

"Mrs. Perkins had her, last I knew. I don't believe they've come down from the mountains yet. Honey, you mustn't feel too bad if the baby isn't alive when they get here. She was awfully weak last time I saw her."

"But she's tried so hard to live. She's so—so stout-hearted, like all the Sagers."

"I know, dearie. Some things in this life we just can't understand." She took Catherine's face between her two rough hands. "You have to be brave, for the others. Now then"—her voice changed to its usual brisk cheerfulness—"let's get you all dressed up in those nice clean dresses. My, but you are a fine-looking lot of children. You must show Mrs. Whitman you've had a good bringin' up. Your ma and pa would want you to be nice to her. She's doin' a lot for you."

Elizabeth threw her arms about Aunt Sally's waist. "I'd rather live with you and Uncle Billy."

"I know, and I wish we could keep you." Suddenly, her face crumpled, and she held her apron to her eyes.

Uncle Billy patted her shoulder. "Now, now, Sally, things aren't as bad as you make out. We'll go down to the valley and find us a house. Next spring I'll come up and get the girls. The boys can come and live with us, too."

58

With this promise in their ears, the four girls climbed into the cart. John and Frank came along behind with the three extra oxen, their old Bossy, and the broken-down cow Aunt Sally had bought. Dr. Dagon cracked his whip and they were off, Uncle Billy leading the way on horseback. The girls, looking out at the back, waved to Aunt Sally as long as they could see her.

Chilled by the sharp October morning, they huddled together under their ragged blankets until the bright sunshine warmed them. Catherine and Elizabeth sat up and peeked through holes in the gray wagon cover to see what kind of country they were going to live in. The trail wound among rolling hills covered with tall, dry bunchgrass. Not a tree broke the skyline.

"I hate it already," Elizabeth said.

"Maybe it will get better as we go on." Catherine was trying hard to be brave as Aunt Sally had suggested, but as the hours went by, she, too, was discouraged by the dreary sameness of the landscape.

"I thought we could make it today," Captain Shaw said, riding up toward dark to talk with the doctor. "These crazy hills, they all look alike. The minute you get around one, another stands in your way. I don't recognize any landmarks, but I think we still have five or six miles to go. We might make it tonight, but we could get lost, too, so let's camp here. We should get there before noon tomorrow."

"Our last night together," thought Catherine, and the boys must have felt the same thing as the six Sagers huddled together in the cart—too sad to laugh, too tired to cry.

Warm sunshine awakened them. The sky was October's special bright blue above the dry weeds along the creek, where red-winged blackbirds darted and scolded. Dr. Dagon had a fire going, and Frank had already milked the cow when the girls climbed out of the wagon. Uncle Billy brought out two slices of bread he had hoarded and divided them. "This will keep you young'uns going till we get to the mission. Then there will be plenty to eat."

Nobody was sleepy this morning. Excitement was in the air. "What do you think the mission will be like, Katie?" Elizabeth asked.

"Oh, I suppose like Fort Hall. It will have a wall around it and blockhouses at the corners and—"

"Indians?"

"Of course. Dr. and Mrs. Whitman are missionaries to the Indians, Papa said."

"What's a missionary?" Matilda asked.

Catherine wrinkled her forehead. "Something like a preacher, I guess."

The long morning dragged away. The children were terribly hungry, but they knew there was nothing more to eat. One thing was hopeful. The road looked more used, and off at the sides, in the tall grass, horses stood grazing.

Catherine looked out of the front peephole just as Captain Shaw rose in his stirrups and waved to someone. Her teeth began to chatter, and she crept back to her sisters, taking Matilda into her lap.

"I don't want to live with Mrs. Whitman. I want to stay with Dr. Dagon," the little girl said, pouting.

"Mama and Papa wanted us to come to Dr. Whitman's."

"I can't remember Mama and Papa."

"Oh, honey, you must not forget them. Don't you remember Papa's beard—how you liked to stroke it?"

Matilda laughed. "It tickled me."

Catherine turned to Elizabeth. "We must not let them forget, Lizzie."

"I'm forgetting, too. I try to remember what Mama looked like and I can't."

A lump rose in Catherine's throat. Not remember Mama? Her soft hair and sparkling eyes?

Uncle Billy rode up to the cart and turned back the ragged cover. "Now you girls watch. You'll see your new home soon."

The road swung around the base of a big hill and entered a broad, level valley. Straight as a string, the trail led toward buildings in the distance. Off to one side, a blue pond rippled in the autumn breeze. Half a dozen white ducks swam there. Catherine was astonished to see that they looked exactly like the ducks on ponds in Missouri.

She saw no walls, no blockhouses. The road passed a square two-story house built of gray adobe bricks, where children played in the yard and women were hanging washing on a line. She saw other buildings, too. That one over there looked like a blacksmith shop. Papa would have liked that. Again, that lump in her throat. Not remember Papa?

A network of ditches full of water led from the pond through a garden where pumpkins lay golden among dry shocks of corn. Beyond the last ditch was a long, low white house with a green door and green window shutters. It might have been a house in Missouri. It looked like a home. A little of the fear and dread melted from Catherine's heart.

Uncle Billy stopped in front of the house, dismounted, and walked up the path to the green door. As it opened, Catherine heard him say, "Mrs. Whitman, your children are here. Will you come out and see them?"

CHAPTER TEN

Dr. Dagon stopped the oxen at the ditch, and the exhausted animals dropped in their tracks, tipping up the cart, so that girls, bedding, and dishes all slid forward.

Captain Shaw called, "Help your sisters out, boys. Find their bonnets."

The boys climbed into the cart and hunted among the litter of clothing and bedding but found only one bonnet, which John tied over Matilda's ragged hair. Frank scrambled over the endgate, untied the ropes that held it, and lifted his sisters out, one at a time. Catherine saw his lips tremble as he held Matilda close in his arms before setting her down. Then he swung around to lean on one of the wobbly old wheels and laid his head on his arms. She knew he was crying.

John resumed his seat, and he, too, began to sob. So the boys knew they were not to stay here. Even Dr. Dagon, standing beside the oxen, whip dangling from his fingers, looked ready to weep. Catherine hugged her sisters together and waited to see the awful person who was separating the family.

At that moment Mrs. Whitman appeared in the doorway, a tall, plump, smiling woman with red-gold hair, a fair complexion, a large nose, and wide gray eyes. She wore a dark blue calico dress and was tying a blue-checked gingham sunbonnet over her head. Catherine, surprised at seeing someone so different from what she had expected, thought she looked like an angel.

For a moment she stood in the doorway, staring at the scene before her as if she could not believe her eyes. Then, picking up her long, full skirt, she stepped swiftly down the path. The girls, like frightened lambs, ran around behind the wagon, turning to peep shyly at her. She stopped at the back of the cart, looked at them a moment, then at the boys, the shocked, unbelieving expression still on her face.

"Why are you crying?" she asked, then murmured to herself, "No wonder, I guess."

As if she still did not know what to say, she began to pull from the wagon some of the tumbled bedding and clothing, shaking each piece free of dust and folding it.

"Help her, boys," Captain Shaw called.

John and Frank ran the backs of their hands over their eyes and once more climbed into the cart, where they handed out the blankets, dresses, and the few tin cups and plates.

A little girl about Elizabeth's size ran from the house, stopped beside Mrs. Whitman, and stared at the children. She looked very pretty in a green dress and white pinafore. Catherine wondered if she could be Mrs. Whitman's daughter. Probably not, since she had dark skin, black eyes, and straight black hair in two braids that hung over her shoulders. Mrs. Whitman gave her a swift hug.

"This is Helen Mar Meek."

Nobody said a word. By this time the clothing and bedding lay in neat piles.

"Take them to the house, boys, if you please. Come, girls."

As Catherine moved from behind the cart, limping badly, Mrs. Whitman exclaimed, "Why, child, you are lame. What happened?"

"The wagon ran over me and broke my leg."

"I'm so sorry. Here, let me help you."

She slipped one arm around Catherine and reached the other hand to Louise. They started up the path, followed by Helen, Elizabeth, and Matilda. Catherine felt kindness in the arm around her shoulders, but all she could think was, "She won't take my brothers." She drew as far from Mrs. Whitman as the circling arm allowed.

At the door, Captain Shaw asked, "Have you no children of your own, Mrs. Whitman?"

Catherine felt the arm on her shoulder tremble and looked up to see bleak desolation in the face above her. Mrs. Whitman nodded toward the foot of the nearby hill, where Catherine could see a standing piece of board, obviously the headmarker of a grave. "All the child I ever had sleeps there."

Tears came to Catherine's eyes as Mrs. Whitman went on, "It is a comfort to me that I can see her grave whenever I come to the door."

"Oh, if only I could see Mama's and Papa's graves," thought Catherine, but she felt more kindly toward Mrs. Whitman knowing that she, too, had suffered loss.

Captain Shaw glanced at Helen Mar. "Then this is not—"

"No, she is the daughter of Mr. Joe Meek. I believe he is a trader. I also have Mr. Jim Bridger's daughter here and a little boy, David Cortez, whose father is Spanish. They all had Indian mothers."

She turned to Dr. Dagon and the boys, who stood waiting. "You passed a house back there beside the road. We call it the mansion house." She smiled, and Uncle Billy laughed, the word was so pretentious for the plain, square house.

"Some of your friends from the wagon train are staying there. You will find a place to wash and to spend the night. Come to supper at five o'clock."

Dr. Dagon bowed. "Danke schön, Frau Whitman. Come, boys."

Captain Shaw also bowed. "I'll see you and your husband later."

As they turned away, Louise shrieked, "John!" and broke away from Mrs. Whitman. John looked around at her, then began to run while Catherine pulled the screaming child into her arms. "John will come back for supper," she whispered.

Inside the house, it seemed dark after the bright light outdoors. When she could see, Catherine noticed another girl about her own size washing dishes.

"This is Mary Ann Bridger," Mrs. Whitman said. "Mary Ann, think you can love so many new sisters all at once?"

Mary Ann smiled shyly.

Mrs. Whitman sat down in a rocking chair, lifted Louise to her lap, and drew the other girls around her. "Now tell me your names and ages."

"I am Catherine, and I am nine and a half. Elizabeth is seven, Matilda Jane five, and Louise three and a half."

"Captain Shaw said something about a baby."

"Yes, Rosanna. Mrs. Perkins had her the last we knew. It might be Mrs. Eads's turn now. The ladies passed her around, you know, to let her nurse when their own babies didn't need all the milk. Their wagons did not come as fast as ours. We don't know—she was so weak—she may be dead."

"Oh. I had hoped—" Her eyes went to a cradle standing beside an inner door.

"Was it your little girl's?"

"Yes. Alice Clarissa's."

"What happened?"

"She drowned in the river. She was two years and three months old." She brushed back her hair as if putting away her

65

sad thoughts. "Helen, run out to the mill and call Father."

Helen dashed away. In a few minutes the door opened, and Catherine saw a man as tall as Papa standing there in a rough gray work shirt and buckskin pants patched in many places. His dark hair was tinged with gray, and he had a dark beard like Papa's. Under shaggy eyebrows, deep-set blue eyes twinkled with fun, and she liked him at first sight. "Well, Mother! What a fine family!"

Louise had managed to slip down from Mrs. Whitman's lap, but when the doctor stooped to pick her up, she shrieked and fled to Catherine. Mrs. Whitman laughed. Catherine thought how much prettier she was when she smiled or laughed.

The doctor looked sheepish, but when he sat down, Matilda went to stand beside his chair. "Here's one that won't scream at the sight of me." Gently he lifted her to his lap. "Light as a feather. What is your name, dear?"

"Matilda Jane."

"What a nice name!" He settled back in the chair, his arm around her. Catherine saw her sister lean against him, raise one hand, and begin to stroke the beard that was so much like Papa's.

"I thought there was a baby," Doctor Whitman said softly.

His wife explained, and he sighed. "Poor little thing!"

"It was the baby I wanted most of all. She would have been more like my own."

"I'm sorry, Mother. We might have been able to save her." He set Matilda on the floor and stood up. "Where are the boys?"

"They went out to the mansion house with Captain Shaw and that man who drove the cart."

The doctor had been looking closely at the children. "Give them just a little bread and milk. They have been starving so long, we'll have to go easy on food."

He hurried away with the quick gait that was to become so familiar to the children. Mrs. Whitman stepped into another room that they were soon to learn was the pantry, where food was kept. She returned with a pitcher of milk and a slice of bread. Their own tin cups stood on the table where the boys had set them. She poured a little milk into each cup and crumbled in some bread. "Now eat slowly. You have not eaten much for some time, have you?"

"No, ma'am," Catherine said. "Nobody had much, but they divided everything they had with us. The whole wagon train sort of adopted us."

"That was good of them. Now the next thing is to give you baths. Mary Ann, you and Helen bring in the tub while I find some clean clothes." She disappeared into the inner room they had not yet seen. Matilda and Louise climbed onto a nearby couch and promptly went to sleep. Catherine and Elizabeth walked around the comfortable kitchen.

"Look, Sis. She has a cookstove!" Elizabeth whispered. "Just what Mama wanted!"

"And cushions on the chairs."

Slowly they circled the large room, almost afraid to speak out loud but nudging and pointing at first one thing, then another: the long table, covered with a clean brown cotton cloth; a small cupboard filled with bottles, probably the doctor's medicine cabinet; books in a wall case; many pots and pans hanging on hooks behind the stove; on a shelf above it, a row of sadirons and candlesticks; a hutch cupboard full of blue-and-white porcelain dishes.

"Oh, Sis, remember Mama's dishes?" Arms around each other, they began to cry as they had not cried since Mama died.

Mary Ann and Helen brought in the wooden washtub. Mrs. Whitman returned, too, her arms full of clean clothes.

She glanced at the tearful girls, then spoke briskly, "Catherine, I'm sure Mary Ann will let you borrow some of her things until your own are washed and mended. Helen's clothes will fit Elizabeth. I've found some outgrown things for Matilda and Louise. Now let's set the tub in the corner behind the stove and put two chairs here with a towel over them for a screen in case somebody comes to the door."

She dipped hot water from a large kettle that always stood on the stove, cooled it from the water pail, and woke Louise. "You're first, little one."

Louise screamed—it had been so long since she had been bathed in a tub. The worst was when Mrs. Whitman washed her head, but after her hair was dry, it shone like silk.

Several times while the older girls bathed, there came a knock at the door and Mrs. Whitman had to answer it. Each time it was some one of the immigrants coming for flour or sugar or medicine.

"This is the way it goes all day long, every day," she said, laughing at the astonished looks on the girls' faces. "You will soon get used to it. We have very little privacy here."

By the time the baths were finished and the soiled clothes put to soak in the bath water, just as Mama used to do, darkness had come. Outside the windows, firelight flickered. Mrs. Whitman explained that some of the immigrants, who were living in their wagons, cooked their food outdoors over campfires.

"It's time I did some cooking, too," she said. She lighted two candles, one for her worktable, near the stove, and the other for the long supper table. She smiled at the girls, who felt strange to be so clean. "You all look nice. A kiss for Mother?"

Catherine solemnly kissed the offered cheek. So did Elizabeth and Matilda. Louise stood back.

"Come give me a kiss, Louise. I am your mother now."

"No."

"Come, I said."

"No."

"Little girls have to mind when Mother speaks."

Louise stamped her foot. "No!"

Catherine saw two red spots flame in their new mother's cheeks, but before she could speak, the door opened and the doctor returned. He laughed at the scene before him, the tiny girl defying the big, angry woman.

"Ha, ha, Mother, who is unpopular now?"

He swung Louise high in the air. She shrieked, but when he set her down, she put up her arms and cried, "Up! Up!"

"Marcus, you interrupted my discipline. She has to learn to obey me."

"Give them time, Mother." He tweaked a loose curl at the back of her neck. "I asked the men to come in for a little private talk after supper."

Behind him came Uncle Billy Shaw, Dr. Dagon, and the two boys. Louise gave a glad cry and threw herself into John's arms.

Mrs. Whitman, still looking a bit miffed, said briskly, "Mary Ann, you and Elizabeth may set the table. Catherine, do you know how to knit?"

"Yes, ma'am."

"Here is a stocking I began last night. You may take it for your work. We waste no time. Even if you cannot walk well, you can keep busy. Sit here by the light."

She moved swiftly around the stove, opening the oven, lifting lids, and moving kettles. Delicious smells floated through the kitchen. Catherine was so hungry that she could hardly keep from snatching a slice of the beautiful brown bread her new mother set on the table. She knew from the expressions on the faces of her brothers as they held the small sisters that they, too, were very hungry.

A boy John's size came in, and Mrs. Whitman introduced him as Perrin Whitman, the doctor's nephew. Tagging after him was a small boy about four years old, Catherine guessed.

"This little tadpole is David Malin." Perrin poked playfully at the boy who was obviously his devoted slave. "Aunt Narcissa found him in a hole in the woods."

. "Now, Perrin, don't tease him." Mrs. Whitman smiled and patted the big boy on the shoulder. "His hands are dirty. Take him outside to the washbench."

When they had gone, she explained, "His mother could not keep him, and his grandmother brought him here. His name is really Cortez, but we call him David Malin for a friend of ours back east. He is a dear little fellow."

When supper was ready, she called everyone to the table, and after the doctor had asked the blessing, he got up to serve the food on each plate. There was baked pork, baked potatoes, mashed turnips, sweet yellow pumpkin that tasted like squash, and the great slices of bread Catherine had been longing for. Butter to spread on them, too.

Again, the doctor gave the children only small portions. Seeing the disappointment in their faces, he said kindly, "You must give your stomachs time to stretch. If you ate as much as you want, you would all be sick." Then he added with a smile, "New pupils for your school, Mother."

"School?" asked Captain Shaw.

"Certainly. In fact, we have two schools, one for Indian children, the other for ours and those of the immigrant families who stay here through the winter. We always have a few of them."

"Who teaches?"

70

Mrs. Whitman broke in, "The doctor and I teach the Indians when any of them are here. They are gone much of the time—to hunt deer, to fish for salmon in the Columbia River, or to work in the camas fields. We may have five pupils or sixty, you never know. We are employing a teacher for the immigrant school, a Mr. Hinman. He came in with an earlier part of your wagon train, Captain Shaw. He seems to be a fine young man and will do well, we think."

Catherine's spirits rose at the thought of going to a real school—just what Mama had hoped they would find in the West.

After supper, Dr. Whitman led the captain and Dr. Dagon back to the inner room the children had not yet seen. The door stood open, so their voices came through clearly to Catherine as she sat near a lighted candle with her knitting. Mrs. Whitman, Mary Ann, and Elizabeth began clearing the table and washing the dishes. They seemed to pay no attention to the voices from the other room.

"But I am supposed to be a missionary to the Indians, not to take care of white people. How can I—"

"You help the immigrants. Seems to me a missionary should look after anyone in need, no matter what the color of his skin," Captain Shaw retorted.

"I don't know whether the American Board will allow—"

"Those are good boys. They would be a big help to you," Dr. Dagon declared.

"Next spring I'll come back and—" Captain Shaw said.

"Perhaps the Eells and Walkers might—"

"Who are they?" Captain Shaw sounded almost angry.

"I am not going to let just anyone have those boys!"

Dr. Whitman broke in. "The Reverend Cushing Eells and the Reverend Elkanah Walker are missionaries sent out by the American Board two years after we came. They opened a mis-

71

sion among the Spokane Indians north of here—place called Tshimakain. Indian word. Means 'valley of springs.' Our place is called Waiilatpu. That means 'place of rye grass.' "

"So that's the stuff growing around here. But now about this American Board. Is that your boss?"

Dr. Whitman laughed. "I suppose you might call it that. It is an organization of the Presbyterian and Congregational churches for sending missionaries to various parts of the world."

"Do they pay you?"

"We receive no pay, Captain Shaw. We are giving our lives in the service to which God has called us. The board allows us a small drawing account at the Hudson's Bay post in Vancouver, but we are supposed to make this mission self-supporting. That is why we have to charge for the supplies immigrants need. Some of them complain at having to pay. We should like to give the supplies free, and we never refuse a man in need if he cannot pay, but we have to charge enough to buy more seed, farming implements, help, and so on. We take nothing for ourselves but food and clothing."

Catherine had listened intently and saw that her brothers, too, were listening. They heard Uncle Billy say, "I'll see you in the morning. Do think seriously about taking the boys."

He and Dr. Dagon came through the kitchen, the boys following them out after John assured the sobbing Louise that he would see her in the morning.

"Time for prayers," Mrs. Whitman announced as she set the last clean dish on its shelf and they all joined the doctor in the sitting room. He opened his big Bible and began to read. This was Catherine's first look at this room. She noticed that it was even larger than the kitchen. A big bed and several couches that could be used for beds lined the walls. A heating stove stood in the middle of the room, but there was no fire in it, and the room seemed chilly after the warm kitchen.

"Catherine, you are not paying attention," Mrs. Whitman said. Catherine felt a hot blush flood her checks. She tried to keep her mind on what the doctor was reading. Then everyone knelt while he prayed. "Time for bed." Mrs. Whitman said as she rose from her knees.

A staircase led up from the sitting room to a big open loft or attic where straw-stuffed pallets, made up with striped gingham sheets, lay on the floor. Each bed had a clean blanket and a clean nightgown folded on top. Mary Ann, Helen, and David went to bunks built against the walls.

"I'll build bunks for you girls as soon as I have time," Dr. Whitman promised. He examined Catherine's weak leg. "Whoever set this did a fine piece of work. Straight as the other one."

"Papa set it."

"Was he a doctor?"

"Not a real one, I guess, but he liked to take care of sick people."

"Your leg will be all right in time. The muscles have become weak from lying still so long."

The two smallest girls were asleep before the doctor and his wife went downstairs.

"Maybe it won't be so bad living here," Elizabeth whispered as she snuggled into her blanket. "Such good things to eat. Mrs. Whitman is awfully pretty, isn't she?"

"She is the prettiest woman I ever saw," Catherine said. "If only they will keep—" She was asleep before she finished the sentence.

CHAPTER ELEVEN

Catherine had barely started down the stairs with Louise the next morning when she heard Dr. Whitman, in the sitting room below, say in a firm voice, "If you want the girls, I want the boys."

"Marcus, I don't see how I can take them."

"Just for the winter?"

A long pause, then, as if with great reluctance, "All right, just for the winter."

"Thank you, Wife."

Catherine wanted to rush on down the stairs, throw her arms around Dr. Whitman's neck, and thank him. However, she was still too much in awe of Mrs. Whitman to do such an impulsive thing, so she walked soberly into the kitchen and said nothing about what she had heard.

All during breakfast she waited for the doctor to make the announcement, but he and Captain Shaw seemed to have much to talk about. Children were to be seen and not heard, so she could not even ask a question that would lead into the subject of the boys' future. The captain ate heartily of the fine beefsteak.

"Good meat. You raise your own cattle, Dr. Whitman?"

"Of course. We raise everything we can except sugar, molasses, and a few other things we buy at Vancouver. We get fish and berries from the Indians. We grind our own wheat and corn. Perhaps you noticed the grist mill. We do not bolt the flour. We think the whole grain is more healthful. That is why our bread is dark."

"I like it. How long have you lived here?"

"Eight years next December." Dr. Whitman replied.

"It is amazing what you have done in such a short time. I never expected to see a large house like this out here in the wilderness. Is it built of logs? The way it is plastered over, I couldn't tell."

The doctor laughed. He laughed easily, Catherine noticed. "I only wish we did have logs, but there is very little timber here in the Walla Walla Valley. We cut enough logs up in the mountains for window frames, doors, and floors, but most of the house is built of adobe brick. Fortunately, we found plenty of suitable clay here. We make the bricks in forms and dry them in the sun."

"Sounds like a lot of work," Captain Shaw observed.

"Everything here is a lot of work. I need all the help I can get." He turned quickly to the boys, who had been sitting with their eyes on their plates, eating hardly anything. "John, Frank, would you like to stay here and be my helpers this winter?"

The boys glanced from one man to another, then to Mrs. Whitman, as if they suspected a joke.

"Do you mean it, Dr. Whitman?" John asked incredulously.

"Indeed I do."

Smiles replaced the sadness in the boys' faces, and Captain Shaw leaped from his chair to shake hands with the doctor. "That is wonderful. You will never regret it."

"I trust not, Captain Shaw," Dr. Whitman said soberly. "Since the children's parents appointed you their temporary guardian, I believe we should make a written agreement. Let us put it down that my wife and I will keep them until spring.

If by that time they are not contented here, or we are not pleased with them, I'll bring them to you in the Willamette Valley. If they do like us and we them, I shall take legal charge of them on my own responsibility." He paused a moment, then added, "Whether the board will make allowance for them or not."

"Thank you both," said the captain. "This was what Henry and Naomi Sager wanted, especially that the children be kept together. Come to see us whenever you are in the valley."

Catherine knew the last link with their old life and with their parents was about to be cut. She managed to keep from crying, but Elizabeth burst into loud wails and threw herself into Dr. Dagon's arms. Matilda and Louise wrapped themselves around his legs and would not let go.

"Come, come, children, this won't do," Mrs. Whitman said. "You want Dr. Dagon and Captain Shaw to remember you crying?" Elizabeth hung her head, and Mrs. Whitman laughed and slipped an arm around her shoulders. "We'll get along all right, won't we, Elizabeth?"

"Any chance of my borrowing a horse for Doc, here?" Captain Shaw asked. "I don't know how we'll get it back to you from our camp over on the Umatilla, but—"

"No trouble," Doctor Whitman broke in. "Leave it with Stickus, my best Indian friend. He will see that it gets back to me." And then they were gone.

That afternoon, Mrs. Whitman and the girls were in the kitchen when a knock came at the door. A woman who looked care-worn and dirty thrust a small, sodden bundle into Mrs. Whitman's arms. "It's my turn to nurse her, but I ain't got enough milk for my own babe. I heard you took the rest of them childern, so I brung her here." She turned on her heel and walked quickly down the path.

Mrs. Whitman laid back a corner of the filthy blanket. A tiny face, like that of a sad old woman, looked up at her. Catherine, who had limped across the room, cried, "It's our baby! And she isn't dead. That was Mrs. Eads."

She hobbled down the path calling, "Mrs. Eads. Mrs. Eads, wait."

The woman turned and waved but did not stop.

"She wouldn't wait," Catherine said when she came back. "I wanted to thank her. Oh, Rosanna, you are still alive."

Mrs. Whitman sat down with the dirty bundle in her lap, and the children crowded around.

"She smells awful," Elizabeth said, holding her nose. Louise struck at the baby, but Catherine drew her away.

"That's our little sister. Will you help take care of her so she'll get well?"

"No." Louise stamped her foot.

"John won't like it if you don't help me."

At the mention of John, Louise looked thoughtful. "I help."

"Catherine, would you hold the baby a minute?" Mrs. Whitman asked. "The first thing we must do is give her some milk. I wish we had a nursing bottle, but perhaps she will drink from a cup."

She brought milk from the pantry and held the cup to the blue lips. The baby swallowed frantically, then up came all she had taken.

"She is even worse off than I thought. A bath will make her more comfortable, then we'll try again."

Mary Ann, who had been watching intently, hurried to fill a basin with warm water from the kettle on the stove and to bring a dish of soft soap. After stripping off the baby's soiled wrappings, Mrs. Whitman let her down gently into the warm water, the first real bath she had ever had. Her wizened face screwed into a wail; then, as she felt the comfort and warmth, she stretched her thin little legs and arms.

"Look, she smiled," Catherine said.

Mrs. Whitman lifted the tiny body to a clean towel laid on her lap. She let Catherine hold her again while she herself went to the bedroom to bring out some of Alice's baby things, carefully laid away five years ago when the little girl died. Clean and dressed in soft clothing, the baby looked more human.

"How old is she?" asked Mrs. Whitman.

Catherine brought Mama's Bible to show the page where names and ages were written. Rosanna's entry was dated May 31, 1844.

"Five months old. No bigger than most babies at three weeks. It is a miracle she is alive."

She brought a little more warm milk in a cup, dipped in one finger, and let a few drops fall into the tiny mouth. The baby sucked the finger as if she never would let go.

"Catherine, keep watch of the time. In an hour, if she keeps this down, give her a few more drops. Can you do that so I can take care of other things?"

"Oh, yes," Catherine replied.

Mrs. Whitman laid the baby in the cradle, and soon she was asleep. Catherine sat beside her with her knitting, joy surging up inside her. Now she could really do something for her baby sister.

The new teacher, Mr. Hinman, was given the extra bedroom next to the kitchen and joined the family for meals. He was a short, chunky man with long dark hair and light, colorless eyes. Catherine felt afraid of him before he had spoken a word, but Mrs. Whitman seemed charmed with him. She kept him next to her at the table and included him in her prayers. Before this, Catherine had looked forward to school; now she dreaded it.

She began to feel terribly alone as well. Frank and John were gone all day, helping the doctor, and her sisters seemed happy playing with the three half-Indian youngsters out in the yard. She could not run and play because of her lame leg, so she was left to watch the baby. She loved Rosanna, she kept telling herself, but outside was beautiful, warm Indian summer weather, though it was November. Catherine had always loved the fall, and she longed to be romping with Elizabeth instead of sitting here giving the baby a few drops of milk every hour. She became so miserable that she cried if anyone looked at her.

"What's the matter with you, Katie?" John asked. "We're all together."

"I know, but everything is so awful without Mama and Papa."

It was Mrs. Whitman who helped her the most. "I have bad times, too, Catherine. Sometimes I go off by myself and cry."

"You do?"

"Yes, I do. You see, I have always had a quick temper, and sometimes it gets away from me. I say things I am sorry for later. That is when I feel so bad I cry."

Looking up at the calm, smiling face, Catherine could hardly believe that sometimes it was bathed in tears like her own.

"Don't tell anyone I told you this. I try to keep it secret." Mrs. Whitman told her.

"I won't." She did not tell anyone, but the little conversation had brought her closer to her new mother. She never felt quite so lonely again.

A few evenings later, the family happened to be alone. No immigrants came to the door, and there were no Indians needing food or medicine. Even Mr. Hinman went to his room to study.

A delightful sense of peace settled over the sitting room where a fire crackled in the fireplace. Dr. Whitman relaxed in a comfortable chair, Matilda on his lap. Catherine and Elizabeth sat on each side of Mrs. Whitman on a settee, all three knitting, while with one foot, Mrs. Whitman rocked the cradle where tiny Rosanna lay sleeping. Already, her little face had begun to fill out, and she looked like a baby instead of an old woman. Louise napped in John's lap, and Frank sat by the fire, whittling a toy horse for watchful David. Perrin was cutting moccasins from leather he had tanned. Mary Ann and Helen, on the floor, murmured softly to their rag dolls.

"Sing to us, Mother," Dr. Whitman urged.

His wife laid down her knitting, slipped an arm around each of the girls, and began a lullaby. It was the first time Catherine had heard that beautiful, rich soprano voice, and it enchanted her.

"Do you like to sing, Catherine?"

"Yes, ma'am, but I don't know how very well."

"We must start a singing class just as soon as I can manage it. Anyone can learn to sing. The Indians did, when we first came here. And the doctor could not even carry a tune until I taught him. Shall we sing one together, Marcus?"

"Not tonight, Mother. I have been studying you as you sit there. You look like a woman who has found the place where she belongs. The Lord knew we needed a family, so He has sent us these children. It is our duty to train them and educate them as well as we can. You cannot do that and continue to work so hard for the Indians. From now on I want you to

80

spend your time with the family. I'll hire someone to help with the housework so the children can have their time for study. One thing I know, I don't want anyone expecting to get them next spring." He held Matilda closer and gave her a kiss.

"Nor do I, Husband. Already, they seem like our own."

Catherine leaned back against the encircling arm, feeling that love surrounded her once more. Someone wanted her. The ache that had been in her throat for so long eased a little. Elizabeth popped up straight, her eyes dancing. "You mean you won't send the boys up to that place in the north? Shimmy-something?"

The doctor laughed heartily. "You mean Tshimakain. And let Mr. Walker and Mr. Eells get the two best helpers that have come my way? I should say not. I think I'll ride over to Umatilla tomorrow, or farther if I have to, and tell Captain Shaw to forget about next spring."

Elizabeth gave a big sigh of relief. "So we are all together again, all seven of us."

"All seven," Mrs. Whitman repeated, looking at the sleeping baby.

CHAPTER TWELVE

Idyllic evenings did not come often to the Whitman family, as Catherine soon learned. At any moment, day or night, an Indian or one of the immigrants might come to the door wanting food, medicine, or help for someone desperately ill. Usually the doctor answered these calls, but if he was away from home, Mrs. Whitman went, even when it meant staying up all night. Such calls had to be answered, despite what her husband had said about devoting her time to the children, yet none of these extra drains on her strength were allowed to reduce the perfection she demanded of herself and the rest of the family. Housekeeping, study, and prayers must follow exactly the rules she had learned from her own mother.

A few months before, she told Catherine, she had been so ill that her husband had not expected her to live. Now, though much improved, she still tired easily, and as the children discovered, she became fretful, impatient, and hard to please. On the other hand, when she was not too tired, nobody could be kinder or more patient. She made rag dolls for the small girls, sang to them, rocked them, and played games with them. No one could help loving her in these good moods.

Dr. Whitman, too, enjoyed being with the children and often took one or more of them with him to visit the Indian lodges. He always carried his Bible and, if the Indians would permit it, talked to them about their sins and need of salvation, though this was something they did not like. Occasionally they would invite him and the children to stay for a feast. To eat with one of their big horn spoons was a special treat.

Time for such pleasures, however, had to be snatched from the constant, unremitting toil in which everyone, including the smallest children, must bear a share. The coming of so many immigrants this year had exhausted the supplies Dr. Whitman had laid up. For his big family to get through the winter, every last pumpkin and squash, every potato—no matter how small—every ear of corn, every carrot, onion, and turnip must be gathered and carried to the cellar under the house. The younger children were given tin cups and told to pick up the white beans that had fallen from split pods when the boys pulled up the dry plants. Mrs. Whitman walked along the rows behind them, and if a single bean had been missed, the child was told, "You might starve next winter for want of that bean. Pick it up."

All the clothing worn by the men as well as by the women and children had to be made by hand, and even a small girl must learn to sew a neat, even seam. Socks, mittens, and caps had to be knitted, and, except for study time, no girl was allowed to sit for even five minutes without her knitting in her hands.

Providing clothes for the seven Sager children added an extra load to the usual sewing in the Whitman house. Everything they had brought with them was worn out or so badly torn that it could hardly be mended, though Mrs. Whitman kept the girls patching as long as there possibility of repair. Patches were no disgrace, she said, only the failure to sew them on. She herself could not do much sewing because her eyesight was poor, but with the help of immigrant women, who were willing to sew in payment for supplies, and the busy fingers of the Sager girls, each child was somehow outfitted with decent clothes before cold weather came.

From time to time, Mrs. Whitman would bring out dresses or shirts from a mysterious barrel that was stored away in her bedroom. Several barrels came every year from a church back east, she told the children, and it was always exciting to open them and see what they contained. Sometimes there would be good, suitable clothing, perhaps a patchwork quilt or even wearable shoes. Other times everything was old and not very clean. But if such garments still held any wear, and if they could be made over, Mrs. Whitman washed and used them.

When the doctor went to Vancouver for supplies, he would bring back, in addition to the barrels, hanks of yarn and bolts of cloth for bed sheets, shirts, and dresses. Often it was stiff, ugly material, but it was the only new cloth they had because Mrs. Whitman did not know how to spin or weave.

Shoes such as the children had worn in Missouri were seldom to be had here in the West. To send east for shoes and get them back would take two years, because all goods came in ships around Cape Horn and up the West Coast. By that time their feet would have outgrown anything ordered, so they all wore moccasins made by Indian women. The girls knitted their own stockings, ripping up old ones to get the usable yarn when no new yarn was available.

With so many beds to be furnished, there must always be quilts in process as well as clothes. Every scrap of new material that did not go into shirts or dresses was carefully cut into pieces of different shapes and sewed into quilt blocks. When enough blocks were ready, Mrs. Whitman spread them on the floor to place the colors in the most pleasing combinations. Then the blocks were sewed in strips and the strips in long seams to form a bed-sized quilt top. Old sheets, neatly patched, were used for the backs. Cotton batting brought up from Vancouver made the filling, and the whole quilt was sewed together in patterns of fine stitching. A new quilt was a treasure indeed.

While the girls sewed, knitted, mended, and quilted, John and Frank helped cut and haul wood, often from a long distance, since trees were scarce in this area. All the water the family used had to be carried from the river, and this, too, was the boys' job.

In order to accomplish all these things in the limits of each day's time, there had to be order and strict rules. Any child could see that, whether he liked it or not. But the children could also see that no one worked as hard or for such long hours as the doctor and his wife, who were up at four o'clock every morning, an hour before the children.

Mrs. Whitman had a passion for cleanliness. To her it came second only to righteousness, and according to Frank, who spent much time at the mansion house, some of the immigrants laughed at her for it. Why change shirts and underwear so often, they scoffed. Why weekly baths? Didn't she know that bathing in winter was dangerous to the health? Did she want them all to take pneumonia? If she heard these remarks, Mrs. Whitman paid no attention to them. The washtub used for bathing was brought into the kitchen once a week, just the way Mama used to do back in Missouri, and the whole family had to go through it.

Then there were the huge weekly washings. By the time Catherine came downstairs at five o'clock on any Monday morning, kettles were steaming on the stove, and already Dr. Whitman, Perrin, John, and perhaps even the teacher, were standing over barrels half filled with hot soapy water, pounding the soiled clothes with stout sticks that had tin cones fastened to one end. Jokes and laughter filled the room, and Mrs. Whitman seemed to enjoy these Monday mornings as much as anyone. She stood in the middle of the kitchen, telling everyone what to do and keeping them all singing as they worked.

Catherine was not strong enough for hard physical work, so she and Frank had the job of cooking breakfast. By the time it was ready, the washing was finished and hung in the yard to dry. Sometimes Mrs. Whitman would look at the long lines of clean clothes flapping in the wind with a sort of shamed expression on her face. "No wonder the Indians think we are rich."

Since Mary Ann, Helen, and David called the Whitmans Father and Mother, the Sager girls soon began to do the same. Only John and Frank refused. Catherine knew from the look on Mother's face that she was hurt when the boys still called her Mrs. Whitman. It hurt Catherine, too, because she was beginning to love her new mother very much. John did, too, but not Frank, who said she corrected him too often.

"But you know she says it is for your own good."

"How does she know what is for my good?" was Frank's angry reply.

John, in his steady way, always said, "Frank, remember what she is doing for us, letting us stay here with the girls."

The children soon learned that the most important part of life in this home was religion. Their own parents had been religious, but in an easy, comfortable way, very different from the anxious, almost grim manner of the Whitmans.

Every morning and evening they had Bible reading and prayers. Before breakfast, each child must learn a verse from Scripture and remember it until Sunday. When that day came, all the playthings and toys, even the baby's rattle, must be put away.

John and Frank openly resented having to go to so many prayer meetings. Sometimes Frank stayed away, but then Mother made special prayers for him later when he was present. He resented this, too.

One thing that interested all the children was roaming through the house, which was shaped like a capital letter T. The sitting room took the middle space, in the crossbar, with the Whitmans' bedroom at one end and at the other a large room that had an outdoor entrance leading into it. The Indians came here for school and church but were not allowed in any other part of the house.

"Why is that?" Frank wanted to know. "They let us go into their lodges—why can't they come into our house?"

"You don't understand, Frank," Mother explained. "They are very dirty and have vermin in their clothing and hair. And if we let them into the rest of the house, we would have no privacy at all."

The long stem of the T began with the kitchen, which backed up to the sitting room. Beyond it was the teacher's bedroom and a storeroom, then the schoolroom that had only an outside door to give the children the feeling of going to a separate school building. Beyond the schoolroom, the doctor planned to add more storage space and perhaps another bedroom to accommodate visitors. Only the crossbar of the T was two stories in height, and so far the second floor was one big room. Father said someday he would divide it with partitions so the boys and girls would have separate apartments. To the Sager children, who had always lived in one-room houses, this seemed like a palace.

Almost every day, at some free moment, the girls and Frank gathered around John to tell him of their joys and sorrows. He seemed more like a father than a brother. He listened patiently, never scolded, but tried to help them accept this life so different from that of their own home. One night he surprised the girls by saying, "Frank and I think it would be nice if we changed Rosanna's name."

"What would we call her?"

"Why not Henrietta Naomi, for Pa and Ma?

"Oh, John, that would be lovely. Papa and Mama would like that."

Father and Mother Whitman agreed. "A real tribute to your parents," Mother said. "We must begin calling her Henrietta now, so she and all of us will be used to it."

That evening when Catherine helped the baby drink her milk, which she now did very nicely from a small cup, she whispered to her, "Your name is Henrietta Naomi Sager. Now you remember that."

The newly named baby laughed. She was growing so fast, Mother said she would soon be as large as Louise. She was everybody's darling, and Catherine wondered how they could have lived without her.

CHAPTER THIRTEEN

As soon as all the immigrants who were not going to spend the winter here had gone on to the Willamette Valley, Mother announced that school would begin. Perrin and John were deemed too old for school, and, besides, the doctor needed them. All the rest, even Louise, would be regular scholars. Mother told them that the teacher, Mr. Hinman, was to have full charge, and they must obey him without question.

From the first day, Frank was in trouble. Mr. Hinman demanded steady concentration on their work. To look up and smile at someone across the room was a sin, and he lost no time letting the sinner feel his displeasure, conveyed by means of a cane that stood near his desk. Gay, mischievous Frank could not resist sticking a foot into the aisle to trip up another boy or letting a few drops from the water pail drip onto a girl's neck. Even a swift glance from his blue eyes would drive Mr. Hinman into a frenzy, and at the slightest provocation, he had Frank up in front of the class for punishment.

Catherine always hid her eyes. If only Frank would yell as other boys did, the teacher might not be so cruel to him, but Frank refused to cry out. Day by day, the struggle between them grew worse. Other boys were beaten, but none so often or so mercilessly as Frank. Mr. Hinman seemed to take pleasure in keeping all the children in a state of terror. Catherine and Elizabeth indignantly told John how their brother was being treated, but he commanded them to keep still. They must not mention it to Mrs. Whitman.

"Anyhow, she would not believe you," Frank said bitterly. "She thinks the teacher is such a fine man that she would not believe a thing against him."

So when Mr. Hinman sat at the table with them, Catherine and Elizabeth kept their eyes on their plates. Mother even commended them for their good behavior. Matilda loved Frank more than anyone else in the world and longed to tell Father what had happened in school, but when she glanced up, she saw Mr. Hinman's hard, gooseberry eyes fixed on her and was so terrified she did not dare speak.

"We are all together—that is the important thing," John reminded them later when the children were all alone. "Frank must learn not to play tricks or laugh or even smile when the teacher is around."

Frank scowled. "I know what I'll do, I'll run away."

"Frank, you wouldn't," Catherine begged.

"Just you wait and see."

The school week ran from Monday morning to Saturday noon. The rest of that day was a half-holiday. The good weather lasted long this year, so on several of these Saturday afternoons Mother took all the children except Catherine for a ramble over the hills. Catherine became used to staying home and consoled herself by reading while she watched the baby. She specially loved the books of poetry she found in the doctor's bookcases and memorized many of the poems.

Just before dark, Mother and the others came home, red-cheeked, smelling of fresh air, and hungry for the Saturday night supper of baked beans, brown bread, and pumpkin pudding, like those both parents remembered from childhood. Early darkness brought a long evening after supper.

Sometimes Father entertained the children with stories of his own boyhood in Rushville, New York, and his later years in Connecticut, where, after his father's death, he had gone to live with an uncle, Freedom Whitman. His grandfather lived there, too, making it a household of men.

"That was when you became so careless about your clothes," Mother teased.

"Perhaps," he said with a sly wink for the children. "Anyhow, my uncle could bake the best beans in the world."

"Better than mine?"

"Yours are good, Wife, but there was just a little something—some trick of seasoning, perhaps—"

"Marcus, you're teasing me."

Catherine thought, as she often did, how pretty Mother was when she laughed. At times like this, she seemed to throw off her customary seriousness and become again the fun-loving person she must have been before she married Father and came west to be a missionary.

She told the children of her own youth in Prattsburg, another New York town, which seemed as far away as China, and when she described her brothers and sisters, Harriet, Phebe, Jane, and Edward in particular, and the fun they used to have, it was for Catherine a glimpse into another world. Could Mother really have been that girl of whom her own mother said, "I wish Narcissa would not always have so much company?"

Matilda and Louise liked best the evenings when Father made shadow pictures for them. He set a candle where it would throw his shadow on the wall, then began to twist his fingers into all sorts of shapes. On the wall appeared a rabbit with long ears, a squirrel, a frog, or a dog opening and closing its mouth until one half expected to hear it bark.

During the week, when Mr. Hinman was in charge of the children for many hours of each day, Mother had more time not only for her housework but also for letter-writing, her favorite occupation. If she was not disturbed, she would sit at the table for hours writing in her fine, even script across the paper one way, then turning it to write the other way. Catherine wondered how her family could read it, but paper was so scarce that cross-writing was necessary if one wanted to say as much as Mother did. She told the children she was urging her parents and her sister Jane to come west.

Whenever a traveler stopped at the mission on the way east, she put aside everything else to finish her letters, asking him to post them when he came to the United States. And whenever anyone arrived from the East, the first thing she wanted to know was, "Are there any letters for me?"

One day she asked Catherine, "Do you remember any relatives your parents had?"

"Mama had a sister, Aunt Hannah."

"What was her last name?"

Catherine shook her head, and neither John nor Frank could remember anything but Aunt Hannah. They had heard Papa speak of sisters and brothers somewhere in Ohio, but where they lived or what their names were they did not know.

"Didn't they ever write letters?"

"I guess not," John said.

"Too bad. I wish we could let them know about you."

Catherine and Elizabeth whispered together at night about this matter of relatives. Wouldn't it be wonderful if, someday, an aunt or uncle came west and stopped to see them? But it was not likely, they guessed.

In spite of the Whitmans' efforts to keep their children away from the Indians, Frank made friends with the Cayuse boys and sometimes spent the night in one of their lodges. He was very quick to learn the Indians' language and before long could understand everything they said. He told the rest of the children they did not like Dr. Whitman because he worked all the time and tried to make them do the same. Men should not work—that was for women. Men were supposed to fish and hunt; when that was done, they had the right to lie around in the sun, smoking and playing the stick games Dr. Whitman said were wrong.

Another reason they disliked him, Frank said, was that he would never parley with them. He insisted on instant answers, yes or no, while they liked to talk all around a subject before making a decision. Neither did he have any feeling for ceremony. He was always in a rush while they never hurried unless they were going on a hunt. They disliked Mrs. Whitman, too, saying she was proud and haughty and would not let her children play with theirs.

No matter how they shunned any kind of farming themselves, the Cayuse did like the watermelons and pumpkins the doctor raised, climbing over the fence at night to steal them. One time, Mother told the children, when Mr. Gray, the missionary who had built the mansion house, was living here, he got so mad at the Indians for stealing his melons that he plugged several growing near the fence and put in some medicine that would make anyone eating them sick to their stomachs. The Cayuse thought they had been poisoned.

She said it was a mistake for Mr. Gray to have done such a thing because the Indians would not forget it and would blame the doctor for it. They had a rule among themselves that if one of their own medicine men did not cure a sick person and that person died, the relatives had the right to kill the medicine man. She was always afraid they would kill Father when his remedies did not cure the patients. She did not worry too much about him when he was home since she did not think the Indians would come into the house to attack him. Often, however, he was called away to one of the other mission stations, and on the way he would be fair prey.

Lapwai, where the Spalding family lived, was a hundred and twenty-five miles to the east, and Tshimakain, home of the Walkers and Eells, a hundred and sixty miles north. The three stations were the points of a huge triangle in which Dr. Whitman was the only physician, and since all the mission families were young people, someone was always having a baby or had a child dangerously ill with whooping cough or scarlet fever. A messenger would come on horseback and the doctor must go, no matter what the weather or how much he was needed at home.

When he started out, his wife knew he might be gone for several weeks. He had to ride horseback, alone, over open country, with no roads but Indian trails, and ford dangerous rivers where a slip of his horse might throw him to his death. In winter, snow hid familiar landmarks, and every foot of the way there was danger, but most of all Narcissa Whitman dreaded the nights that he was away. Often she asked Catherine to sleep with her. She seemed to forget this was only a ten-year-old child and poured out to her all the troubles of her heart. Catherine was a willing and sympathetic listener.

Once, in the middle of a dark, cold night, the two of them were awakened by weird cries from the Indian camp nearby. Catherine began to tremble, and shivers ran up her back.

"What is that awful noise?"

"The death chant. Someone must have died. I wonder who it is. I am almost glad the doctor is away. They would

94

have come for him, and then, when the patient died, they would have blamed him for it."

The cries continued all night. In the morning a weeping Indian woman came to the door. When she had gone, Mother turned swiftly. "The sick man is the son of one of the chiefs. He is not dead yet, but they think he is dying. Mary Ann, run down cellar and bring me two large onions."

She built up the fire, sliced the onions into a pan of water, and set them to cook. As the room filled with the pungent fumes, she spread out on the table a strip of old flannel, topped by a rectangle of worn cotton cloth. As soon as the onions were thoroughly heated, she spooned them onto the cloth and folded it with the flannel strip around it.

"Catherine, will you come with me to the Indian camp?"

Catherine shivered. "But, Mother, if the man dies, won't the Indians kill us?"

"Our lives are in God's hands," she replied.

They wrapped shawls around their heads and shoulders and set forth in the snow. At the Indian lodge, Mother went straight to the side of the sick man, who lay on a buffalo robe, gasping for breath. She opened his buckskin shirt and clapped the hot onion poultice on his chest and neck, binding it with the strip of flannel. He choked and struggled, but she held him firmly until he calmed down. Then, she spoke a few words of instruction to the weeping women standing around and beckoned to Catherine. On the way home she said, "He has quinsy. His throat was swelled almost shut."

They had reached the house when she stopped and held up one finger. "Listen."

"What is it, Mother?"

"Haven't you noticed? The death chant has stopped. He

must be breathing better. I thought he would. Nothing like an onion poultice." She smiled mischievously, and Catherine found it hard to remember that this was the same woman who had been so frightened in the night.

Some of the immigrant children in the school began to talk about Christmas. The Sager children had always loved Christmas in Missouri. Papa came of a German family who had made much of the holiday in the old country and had brought their customs with them. The children had hung up their stockings before the fireplace and in the morning found them stuffed with presents—simple gifts, made by Papa and Mama, but they carried the magic of Christmas. Papa made taffy, which he pulled over a hook, and they sang German carols and had a jolly time. With these pleasant memories in mind, Catherine timidly asked Mother if they might hang up their stockings on Christmas Eve as the immigrant children were going to do.

"Christmas is a pagan celebration," Mother said sternly. "We'll have none of that in this house."

Catherine crept away feeling as if she had done something terribly wrong. Her brothers reacted angrily when she told them what Mother had said. All day on December twenty-fifth Frank sat glumly in his seat in the almost empty schoolroom and hardly spoke at meals.

Only a week later, on New Year's Day, things were different. Mother and Father believed this was a day for enjoyment and for starting all over again. Mother cooked a feast with mince pie for dessert. She had saved some of the dried apples Father had bought in Vancouver and put in a few raisins as well. The family so seldom had either cake or pie, the meal was a great treat.

It would have taken more than mince-meat pie to raise Frank's spirits in the new year, however. As the months passed, Mr. Hinman continued to beat Frank, while Mother told the girls that their progress in reading, spelling, and arithmetic proved that he was a fine teacher. John still urged Frank to hang on for the sake of keeping the family together, but as February turned to March and March to April, Catherine knew her younger brother was nearing the end of his endurance.

CHAPTER FOURTEEN

Overnight, it seemed, the bushes along the creek wrapped themselves in gowns of the loveliest green in the world; the cottonwoods by the river and Father's young apple trees put out dancing clouds of tiny leaves; all over the hills that surrounded the Walla Walla Valley the new bunchgrass sprang up like emerald velvet. Red-winged blackbirds, mountain bluebirds, and bold, speckled flickers darted through the trees and the tall rye grass along the fences. Catherine thought she had never seen so lovely a spring.

Mother explained that every year all the members of the Oregon Mission, unless they were ill, came together at one or another of the three stations for a business meeting, baptism of children, and admission of church members if there were any candidates. The missionaries, especially the women, saw one another so seldom that the annual meeting was a reunion and social gathering as well. This spring it was to take place here at Waiilatpu.

Mother began housecleaning with furious energy, the way she said her mother had always done in spring. Every straw tick had to be emptied, washed, and refilled with fresh, clean straw, and extra ones prepared for guests. Every wall must be brushed down, every window washed, every piece of furniture polished, every floor cleaned to the last crack. The girls had never worked so hard in their lives, but when it was done, the house smelled so sweet and clean that it was worth all the work.

The coming of warmer weather also brought activity outside the house, where Father and the boys spaded up Mother's garden so she could plant the flower seeds she had carefully saved from last year. Mama used to like flowers, too, Catherine remembered, yet somehow, this spring, she found it hard to remember Mama and Papa. The younger girls never mentioned them any more, not even Louise, who had cried for Mama every night for so long.

Spring also inspired the immigrants who had spent the winter here. They were busily repairing and loading their wagons for the journey to the Willamette Valley. It almost seemed that everyone was leaving Waiilatpu, for the Indians, too, were packing up for their annual trek to the fishing grounds along the Columbia River, where the salmon run would soon begin. Catherine noticed that Frank spent all his free time at the mansion house these days, and she wondered if he might really be planning to go with one of the wagons as he had threatened.

One night Father was called away to the Umatilla to see some sick Indians and Mother conducted evening prayers. Afterwards Frank pulled Catherine away from the others, out into the warm darkness.

"Sis, I am leaving tomorrow with the Howards."

"Oh, Frank, no."

"I have to. I can't stand it any longer—either the teacher or Mrs. Whitman. I can never please her no matter what I do."

"What does John say?"

"I don't care what he says. The Willamette Valley is where Pa was going to take us, so that is where I am going. Don't tell Mrs. Whitman."

"I won't, but please, Frank, don't go."

She thought surely Frank would not leave, but when she came downstairs in the morning, he was gone. Mother immediately sent John and an Indian to look for him, but when they returned long after dark, they had not found him. In the morning she asked John to go again, and again he came back without Frank.

"I think he must have left with the wagons," John said.

When Father came home and heard the news, he said quietly, "I've been afraid this would happen. I tried to tell the teacher—" At the look on Mother's face he stopped and did not mention the matter again.

For days, the house seemed so empty and lonesome that Catherine felt as if someone had died. Only now did everyone seem to realize how much Frank's smile, his happy ways, and lighthearted mischief had meant in their daily life.

The mansion house stood empty and deserted now. Nobody came to the house for food or medicine; no children ran screaming about the yard. The valley among the great hills became the lonesomest place in the world. Even the raucous shouts from the Indian camp would have been a relief, but they, too, were missing, and where the tepees had stood was only empty space. Nevertheless, Mother insisted they must go on with their usual work, so all were up early, toiling in the garden now that it was planting time. She gave each girl a small space for her own where she could plant whatever she wished, provided she would water and weed it herself.

At first they talked of Frank every day, but gradually the void he had left seemed to fill in. Yet to Catherine, something was always lacking. Often, when she was stirring the soup for supper, with the kitchen door open because of the summer heat, a shadow would fall across the doorway and her heart would jump in glad expectation. Frank! But it never was he. She wanted to go out into the hills and shout, "Frank, where are you? Why don't you send us a letter?" It was the silence that seemed so awful.

When the weather grew warm, Mother said they might as well bathe in the river to save carrying water. Wearing their oldest dresses, with nothing underneath, the girls followed Mother through the orchard to the river. Here, she told them, was where Alice had drowned, so they must be very careful. She selected a shallow place and waded in, ducked under, and came up shivering and laughing. With many squeals, the girls did the same. Even Henrietta was dipped, and they all ran back to the house for a quick rubdown before the good dinner Mother had left simmering on the stove.

"Now, wasn't that fun?" she asked.

Elizabeth shivered. "It was awfully cold."

"You'll get used to it and like it as I do. It was what helped me get over my illness last year. We'll bathe every day."

During the spring days that followed, everything seemed so peaceful that it was a surprise when old Stickus, Father's best Indian friend, came riding up to the house one day and talked a long time. After he had gone, Father told the family what he had said.

Some weeks before, a band of Cayuse, reinforced by a few Spokanes and Walla Wallas, had gone off to California, driving a band of horses to trade for cattle. Their destination was a place called Sutter's Fort on the Sacramento River. There, Stickus said, they had quarreled with some white men and the son of the leading Walla Walla chief had been killed. The Indians had panicked, abandoned their horses, and fled. They were now on their way back with the intention of avenging the young man's death by killing two white men, Father and Archibald McKinley, Chief Factor of the Hudson's Bay Company at Fort Walla Walla.

John and Perrin were greatly excited and began to overhaul all the guns on the place. One of them, John discovered, was the very gun Papa had owned, that had been stolen from Mama and later traded to Father. For a moment, Mama and Papa seemed real again.

Father said he could not blame the Indians, but he felt sure the cooler heads among them would have calmed them down before they reached Fort Walla Walla.

"Not a very good time to have a mission meeting." Mother declared. "What if they kill us all?"

Father smiled and patted her shoulder. "You don't know our Indians as well as I do, my dear. Just go ahead and get things ready for the meeting."

The twelve missionary guests arrived on the eighth of May. Five were adults, the Eells and the Walkers from Tshimakain and Mr. Spalding from Lapwai. Mrs. Spalding's newest baby was too small to travel, so Mr. Spalding brought only his daughter, Eliza, who was about Elizabeth's age. The four little Walkers and the two Eells children mingled joyously and noisily with the younger Sagers until the house seemed to be rocking. Since there was no one of Catherine's age, she spent her time taking care of Henrietta.

After the meeting ended, Father made plans for his annual journey to Fort Vancouver, to bring back supplies he had ordered from the East one or two years before. "This year I am ordering a threshing machine and a corn sheller," he announced. "The way people are pouring into this country, I'll need to raise a lot more wheat and corn. Hand-threshing and shelling are too slow and hard."

This year he would have a traveling companion on his trip, for Mr. Hinman had decided to leave the mission school for the Willamette Valley. Mother seemed sad to see him go, but the girls and John had difficulty concealing their delight when their tormentor actually mounted his horse and rode away.

When Father returned from Vancouver, he told the children that he had called on Captain Shaw in the valley and had appeared before a judge who appointed him their legal guardian. "So now that I really am your father, you must wear these things I have brought you."

From his saddlebags came handkerchiefs, ribbons, and circle combs for the girls to use to hold back their fine hair. For the boys, there were new caps and pocket knives, and for all delicious candy, horehound drops, lemon drops, and peppermint sticks. For the school, Father brought new books, slates, and slate pencils and a wonderful big map of the world to hang on the wall. It was like Christmas in Missouri.

"Did you hear anything about Frank?" Mother asked.

"I saw him and talked with him. He looked fine."

"But you couldn't persuade him to come back?"

"I didn't try. He has to make his own decision. I told him we love him and want him, but I will not force him."

Mother turned away, looking as if she would cry. "He will never come," thought Catherine. "Oh, Frank, will I ever see you again?"

Then, one day in the early fall, who should come riding up the road but Frank, looking taller and older than when he went away. He seemed a little cautious about coming into the house, but when Mother flung her arms around him and cried, "Oh, Frank, I'm so glad you are home again," the scared look left his face.

Not that there was no more trouble, but little by little Mother eased her rules, and the feeling between them became less strained. One day, months after his return, he said, "Mother—" then stopped.

A surprised, happy look came over her face. "Frank, you called me Mother."

He laughed. "It's as good a name as any, I guess."

CHAPTER FIFTEEN

Now began for Catherine what she would always remember as two of the happiest years of her life. The discipline of the Whitman home had become well established, and life moved in a smooth pattern of home, school, and church, all under the same roof.

Andrew Rodgers, the teacher who replaced Mr. Hinman, was as different from him as day from night. Tall, fair, an good-looking, he had smiling blue eyes and a humorous mouth. In no time he had won the children's confidence and admiration.

Mother was specially pleased because he had a fine voice and played the violin well. He took over the singing class and organized the children into a choir for church and for entertaining guests.

Many travelers came through Waiilatpu that fall. After supper Mother would line up her "stairway" of children with tall Perrin at one end and tiny Henrietta at the other. To the accompaniment of Mr. Rodgers' violin, they sang in full harmony, delighting themselves and enchanting listeners. Henrietta, though not yet two years old, could already carry a tune, and when visitors made a big fuss over her, Catherine was as proud as if she had been her mother.

If Father and Mother worried about the Indians, they kept it to themselves. As far as the children were concerned, especially the girls, Indians were only part of the background of their lives, seen but not felt. Now and then, however, they sprang a surprise.

The Indians were in the habit of bringing their corn and wheat to Father's grist mill to be ground into meal and flour, and Father treated them as he would have anyone else, first come, first served. One busy morning, however, Tomahas, one of the chiefs, demanded service at once without waiting his turn. When Father would not let him have his way, he became very angry and stormed off, threatening revenge.

At dinnertime, Father and the miller stopped the machinery and came to the house. In the middle of the meal a terrible racket sounded from the mill, as if it were falling apart. The miller jumped up and ran out with Father right behind him and the children trailing after. As they reached the mill, Tomahas stepped out and knocked the miller flat, then dashed toward Father. Before he could reach him, another chief, Teloukaikt, who was one of Father's friends, appeared suddenly and grabbed Tomahas around the waist. The man raged and fought, but Teloukaikt was stronger. In Indian, he said to Tomahas, "I'll let you go if you promise to leave and make no more trouble."

Tomahas sullenly agreed, mounted his horse, and rode away. Father and the miller found that he had filled the hopper with sticks, which had made the noise when he started the machinery. When the family returned, Mother rushed, weeping, into Father's arms. He patted her shoulder. "It was nothing, my dear, nothing at all."

"That Tomahas—I'm afraid of him."

"Teloukaikt can handle him," Father replied.

More children were added to the family this fall when Cyrus Walker and Eliza Spalding came to spend the winter and go to school. Mary Johnson, from one of the immigrant families, was also eager for education, so she joined the Whitman clan, working for her room and board and schooling. She seemed like an older sister to the Sager girls, and they grew very fond of her.

With a family like this, something was always happening that scared Mother half to death, she said. There was, for instance, the Monday morning when some of the dirty clothes had not been brought downstairs, and she gave Helen Mar a candle to light her way up to look for them. Helen returned with a few clothes but no candle.

"Did you blow it out?" Mother asked.

"No, I stuck it in that keg of black sand at the head of the boys' bed, and I am going back to look for the rest of the washing."

Mr. Rodgers took the stairs three at a jump while Mother stood frozen and pale until he brought back the candle. Only then did the children learn that the black sand they had uncovered and been playing with was gunpowder.

All in all, however, the winter passed pleasantly with everyone well and not even much sickness among the Indians. The weather was so mild that as early as February the trees began to put out their new leaves.

Father had given Perrin, John, and Frank horses of their own, and often on Saturday afternoons in the spring they brought them up for the girls to ride. Sometimes Mother rode with them. John carried her old sidesaddle from the barn, and she put on the gray pongee riding habit in which, she told the girls, she had ridden all the way across the plains in 1836, just ten years ago.

She began to teach the children botany, and one warm day she suggested a picnic so that they could gather wildflowers to mount and classify. She packed a lunch and her good blue-and-white dishes in a small cart Frank had made. She rode horseback, with Henrietta in front of her, while the rest walked. By now Catherine's leg had improved so much that she could easily keep up with the others.

They wandered up Mill Creek, so named for Father's mill, until they came to a pleasant place with trees and grass, where they spread the lunch. When Elizabeth's plate was empty, she turned it over and spelled out a name on the back, "S-P-0-D-E."

"What does that mean, Mother?"

"It is the name of the company in England that made these dishes."

"Our dishes came from England?"

"Yes, they did. Of course we bought them in Vancouver, at the Hudson's Bay Company store, but they bring everything from England."

"I should think you would have brought tin dishes on a picnic." Elizabeth said.

"I want you children to get accustomed to nice things and to handling them carefully."

After the meal they put the dishes in the cart and started home. On the way Elizabeth and Helen noticed a wasp's nest, and when the girls made a game of throwing clods at it, the wasps swarmed out to attack their human enemies. Helen was stung on one knee and Frank, who was pulling the cart, on his face and hands. Instinctively he began to run, and as the cart bumped clumsily over the rough trail, two of the lovely Spode plates were tossed out and broken. Worse than that, the wasps attacked Mother's horse, making it rear and plunge until she and Henrietta were almost thrown off. When they reached home, she called the children together. "Who threw the clods?" she demanded.

Elizabeth hung her head, and Helen spoke up bravely. "Elizabeth and I did, but I threw first."

"Up to bed and no supper," Mother commanded, pointing sternly toward the stairs.

"Oh, now, Mother," Father broke in. "They meant no harm. We can buy more plates."

Mother's cheeks grew red. "You leave the disciplining to me and then you upset it." Suddenly she laughed. "Oh well, I should have taken tin plates."

The children tried not to smile, but they knew Father found them amusing and adored him for it.

When school ended and the Spaldings came to take Eliza home, Mother decided she and the girls would go a few miles with them and camp overnight. Frank drove the oxcart with David for male companionship. Six or seven miles up the river they came to a beautiful spot beside the swift-flowing Walla Walla River, where the trees and blooming wild flowers made a real garden. After the Spaldings had gone on, the children waded in the river while Mother cooked supper. They ate around the campfire with much laughter and singing, then rolled up their blankets for the night.

The next morning the oxen were gone, and Frank and David set out to find them while the girls settled down for another day of fun. By noon, however, their food was gone and they were hungry. "Let's catch some fish," Elizabeth said. "I see plenty of them in the river."

"But we haven't any hooks or lines," Catherine replied.

Just then, a band of Indians, mostly boys they knew, came along the trail, laughing and joking among themselves. They called out to the girls, who waved at them, and the idea of fishing was forgotten by all but Elizabeth, who left the others and walked by herself along the river. She could see beautiful salmon swimming in the clear water and longed for a hook and line. Suddenly she spied a big fish caught between two rocks at the edge of a pool and instantly pounced on it. Slippery and wriggling, it was almost more than she could lift, but she held on to it, wrapping her soaking dress around it.

Elizabeth was just turning back toward the camp when, from nowhere, a hand came down over her shoulder and snatched away the fish. She looked up to see an Indian boy grinning as he held the salmon above her head. "That's my fish! You give it back!" she shouted.

For answer, he raised it higher, but the leader of the band, a Delaware Indian named Tom Hill, who had recently appeared among the Cayuse, spoke sternly to the boy, who looked ashamed and gave back the fish. The Indians went on their way, and the girls and Mother had a salmon feast before the boys returned with the oxen.

Father laughed when he heard about the fish episode. "That Tom Hill has become an important man among our Indians. He lived with the Nez Percés for several years, I hear. Kept telling them how the white men had driven his tribe out of their homes and would do it here, too. He's right, of course. That's why I want so much to help them learn to farm, for the days will come when their hunting grounds will be gone."

"He speaks English very well," Mother said.

"Yes, he has been well educated. If I could make friends with him, he would be a big help to me. The Indians seem to set great store by what he says."

The summer of 1846 passed quickly and uneventfully. By that fall, Mr. Rodgers had decided to study for the ministry and gave up teaching, asking to remain as a boarder. Although the children all felt sad to lose him, the new teacher, William Geiger, was a fine young man from Mother's own home town and church.

Eliza Spalding came back to school, bringing her little brother Henry, who was only six years old. Mother was not pleased to have so young a child added to her family, but she could not refuse her friends the Spaldings.

Now the family who sat down for meals three times a day numbered eighteen, in addition to frequent guests—explorers, scientists, military men, or adventurers. Mother was indeed fortunate to have Mary Johnson to help her with the cooking.

To all the guests, Father remarked how very peaceable the Indians seemed this year. "They are beginning to find out how much better they can live by doing a little farming," he explained, but Catherine overheard him say to Mother, "I feel terribly discouraged. Tomahas says the Indians want us to leave."

"Where could we go, Marcus?"

"There is talk that the Methodists want to sell their station at The Dalles. We could live and farm there as well as here. Many of the immigrants now go straight across country to that point anyhow."

"It is too late to go this fall. Wagons will soon be coming."

"Yes, of course. We can't move this year, but I am thinking of next year."

Catherine wondered if they really were going to move, but Father did not mention it again. He was soon occupied with packing supplies over to the Umatilla for the incoming immigrants, who brought the glad news that the government had made a treaty with Great Britain, setting the Canadian border at the Forty-ninth Parallel.

"One of my dreams has come true; the Oregon country now belongs to the United States," he told the children.

"Where is Oregon?" Catherine asked. "Papa said we were going there."

"What we usually mean by the word Oregon is the Willamette Valley," Father explained. "What the treaty calls the Oregon country is all the territory north of California and west of the Rocky Mountains."

"It must be a big country," Catherine remarked.

"It certainly is. Someday I suppose it will be cut up into states."

Catherine did not hear talk of moving to the place called The Dalles again until spring. The annual mission meeting was to be held at Tshimakain this year, and Mother said she could not take the whole family because the Eells and Walkers didn't have enough room. Only Catherine, who, she decided, needed a rest from her constant care of Henrietta, was allowed to go, and because there were no children her age to play with, she was permitted to listen to the discussions.

The main subject was the Methodist property at The Dalles. "I think we ought to buy it and set up a new mission," Mr. Spalding said. "Who would take charge of it?"

Mr. Walker looked at Father. "Why not you, Dr. Whitman, now that the Cayuse have become threatening?"

Catherine expected Father to agree since he had said almost the same thing at home. To her surprise, he reversed his stand, declaring he was not going to leave Waiilatpu, the place he had worked so hard to build. Let Mr. Walker move.

At this, Mrs. Walker glowered. Though women were not permitted to speak in the meeting, she made it plain that she was not about to be torn from her home, either. Mrs. Walker had strong opinions, and all the men knew it, so they hurriedly agreed to send Father, who lived nearest, to arrange for buying the property. They could decide later who would live there, yet they all seemed upset and apprehensive about the future of the whole Oregon Mission.

Catherine worried a lot about it. Had Father and Mother been keeping something from her and the other children? Did they really expect trouble? But once she was home again, absorbed in the calm, peaceful routine, she forgot all about the problems raised at the meeting.

When school closed, in the spring, Mr. Geiger set off for the valley, and Eliza and Henry Spalding went home. This year John went with them to work for Mr. Spalding through the summer—his first job at man's wages. Mother sent Mary Johnson, too, because Mrs. Spalding's health was poor and she needed help. The family would certainly have seemed greatly reduced if it had not happened that Mr. Manson, a trader for the Hudson's Bay Company, brought his two lively sons to Waiilatpu, asking Mother to keep them for a year.

Father bounced back from his spell of depression and announced that he had definitely made up his mind not to leave Waiilatpu. Instead, he was going to hire men to live at the sawmill next winter and get out timber to build a new house for Mother. They would set it farther back from the river, a little way up the hillside. Striding up and down the sitting room, he declared, "Someday there will be a city here, with schools, an academy, perhaps a college. This valley has a great future. I want to be part of it."

Visitors were not unusual, but the man who rode up from the valley one day was a type never before seen here—an artist. His name was John Mix Stanley. He had been employed by the Smithsonian Institution to make a pictorial record of people and places in the West. He was a wonderful guest, laughing and joking with the children and entertaining Father and Mother with the latest news. They were sorry he could stay only one night, but he promised to come back later. "Maybe paint your pictures," he said, winking at the girls.

Soon another artist appeared, a Canadian named Paul Kane. His ambition was to paint portraits of Indians. Father looked dubious. "They do not like that sort of thing. They have a different idea from ours about pictures. Painting them might lead to trouble."

Unknown to Father, Mr. Kane persuaded Frank to take him to visit the Indian lodges, and at Chief Teloukaikt's home he managed to sketch the Indian without being observed. When they went to the lodge of Chief Tomahas, however, he was not so lucky. He pretended to be interested in the furnishings of the tepee, but all the time he was drawing the features of the chief.

Frank, who reported the incident to his brother and sisters, grinned as he remembered the rage of Tomahas when he saw what the artist was doing. "I think he would have killed Mr. Kane if I hadn't helped him get to his horse and escape."

"But, Frank, won't Tomahas be angry with you for doing that?" Elizabeth asked, but Frank just shrugged.

Mr. Kane proudly showed Father and Mother the sketches. "That Tomahas is the most savage-looking man I've ever seen," he said. "I'm so glad I got these drawings. Now I can reproduce them with paints."

Mother and Father said no more, but Catherine knew they did not approve of what he was doing. Refusing to take their warning, Mr. Kane, the very next day, when an Indian woman came to see Mother, drew her picture on his sketch pad and held it up for her to see. She screamed and tried to snatch it from him. When she could not, she began to weep and wring her hands.

With surprise written on his face, the artist asked, "What is the matter? What is she crying about?"

Mother said soberly, "She says if you keep the picture, it means you have her soul in your power."

"Oh, bosh!"

Mother talked quietly to the woman, and finally she went away. But that was not the end of the artist's mischief. Mother had set the children the job of raking the yard, and Mr. Kane went out to watch them. When they saw he was drawing their pictures, Matilda, in a playful mood, upended her rake and tried to balance it on one finger. Mr. Kane quickly sketched her in this pose before Mother appeared at the door, the familiar red spots of annoyance in her cheeks. "Matilda, stop that nonsense and get to work. I don't want a picture of you acting so foolish."

Mr. Kane only laughed and slipped the picture into his portfolio. Catherine did not tell Mother he had sketched her and Father also when they were not looking. She and her sisters thought it a great joke. Mother seemed glad to bid goodbye to Mr. Kane. After he had gone, she said to Frank, "Don't ever take anyone else to the Indians' lodges."

"Why not? They know me. We are friends."

Mother looked off into the distance, her eyes troubled. "I hope what you have done will not bring danger to you, Frank. The Indians are different from us. Just be careful—that's all I ask."

CHAPTER SIXTEEN

A man coming up from the Willamette one day during the fall of 1847 stopped at the mission to tell Father that the farm machinery he had ordered two years ago had been brought to The Dalles.

"How fortunate!" Father exclaimed. "I hear there are five thousand people coming across the plains, and they will all need supplies by the time they get here. The threshing machine and corn sheller will come in handy."

John, who had returned from Lapwai a few weeks earlier, was preparing to take a pack train back there to bring potatoes and wheat from Mr. Spalding's farm.

"Could you put this off long enough to bring home the machinery?" Father asked, "I have to ride to the Willamette to buy that Methodist property."

"I guess I can," John replied.

"And, Perrin, would you be willing to take charge of The Dalles station this winter?"

Perrin looked surprised but pleased. "Why, sure, Uncle Marcus, if you think I can do it."

"Of course you can. Get ready and ride down with John. You'll need two wagons, one for each machine. I'll send an Indian along to help load the equipment and drive one wagon back."

When Father returned from the valley, he told Mother he had bought the Methodist property for six hundred dollars, a bargain, and he hoped the board would forward the money promptly. He had also found a new route between The Dalles and Umatilla. It was farther back from the Columbia than the old road, more direct and not plagued with shifting sand dunes. He intended to go right back to urge the immigrants to try it.

"I'll take along a load of supplies," he announced. "The first wagons are already coming down from the mountains. You ride over with me, Mother. Perhaps we'll find a good teacher."

"I'd like to have a lady teacher this time," Mother said. "The girls need someone to help them with embroidery and tatting and manners."

"You may be right, but I think we need a man teacher, too."

"And I need a cook since Mrs. Spalding has asked to keep Mary Johnson all winter. Catherine, you come with me to help find these people."

As they stood together beside the trail watching the wagons rumble down the long grade of Emigrant Hill, Catherine could hardly remember when she had looked like these dusty, weary people. Only three years ago? She felt as if she had always lived at Waiilatpu.

At the camp, Mother met a charming young woman named Lorinda Bewley, who she decided was just the one to teach her girls. It was quite a job to induce her to spend the winter at the mission, but Mother could be very persuasive when she wanted to, and when at last she gained Lorinda's consent, she was triumphant. Father, too, succeeded in finding a man named Judge Saunders, who was willing to teach for a year so his four children could have the advantage of a school.

In an exuberant mood, Father went a day's journey along the new road, to point out the way to the lead wagons, but when he returned to Mother and Catherine at the Umatilla, he looked like a different person. Worry lines furrowed his face; his deep-sunk eyes were dark with foreboding.

"Whatever is the matter?" Mother asked.

"There were some sick children in those wagons. Measles. A lot more in the wagons behind, they told me. If this gets to our poor Indians—"

All the brightness left Mother's face, as if a curtain had been pulled over it. "We'd better hurry home and get ready." She explained to Catherine, "The Indians have a favorite remedy for illness. They steam themselves, then jump into the river. It helps some of their diseases, but for measles it would mean death."

Overnight the mission house, which had been so gay and full of hope, turned gloomy. Frank, who circulated among the Indian lodges, brought word that Tom Hill, on whom Father had counted for help, was now telling the Cayuse his old story of what was going to happen to them and stirring their resentment against the white men, especially Father, because he encouraged and helped the settlers.

Another piece of bad news was that a Catholic priest had come to the Walla Walla area and was looking for a place to build a mission. The Indians, Frank said, had offered him the Waiilatpu buildings as soon as they could drive Dr. Whitman away. The priest had refused their offer, but that did not change the fact that they had made it. Catherine could tell that both Mother and Father were alarmed, but they concealed their feelings enough to welcome Lorinda Bewley and the Saunders.

Very soon wagons full of sick children began to arrive. Since the mansion house had four rooms downstairs and five smaller ones upstairs, Mother was able to stow away the first comers by insisting that each family, even those with several children, occupy only one room. As more and more people came, they had to camp in their wagons and cook over outdoor fires. Father had only a few simple remedies for measles. Mostly it was a matter of keeping the children warm and in bed, and after a few days most of them recovered without bad aftereffects.

This was not the case with the Indian children, who soon began to come down with the disease. Mother's prophecy was all too true, for in spite of the doctor's advice and warnings, they used the steam-bath and cold-plunge treatment. The wailing of the death chant became almost constant.

However ill-advised the Indians' methods of treating measles might be, they all loved their children intensely, and as deaths mounted, their anger against the white men increased. Even the Sager children, kept inside the house, became aware of it.

"I'm awfully scared," Elizabeth whispered at night.

"So am I," Catherine whispered back. "I feel so sorry for the poor Indians. Suppose it was our Louise and Henrietta that died."

"Oh, no, Katie. Don't think such a thing."

The epidemic grew worse. Chief Teloukaikt, who so far had been faithful to Father, lost three sons in as many days and became a broken man. He could not conceal his thirst for vengeance. As October moved into November, everyone in the mission could feel the tension in the air.

Tom Hill disappeared, but his place was immediately taken by an ugly fellow named Joe Lewis, who was also part Indian and bitter over the troubles of his people. He lacked Hill's pleasant manner and had been so disagreeable on the journey west that none of the immigrants would have him in their wagons. He arrived at the mission on foot, almost starved and without a shirt on his back.

Although Father, with his customary kindness, supplied him with clothes and food and offered him work, Joe Lewis proved so useless and mean that Father told him to go on to the valley. He left, but in a few days was back, hanging around the Indian camp. Frank kept Father informed of his actions. Lewis, he said, went much further than Tom Hill in trying to arouse the Indians. He told them Father was poisoning them to get rid of them all—he had heard the white men plotting it—and the Indians were not reluctant to believe him. They could see for themselves that white people were not dying, only Indians.

The mission was so gloomy and full of foreboding that nobody paid much attention when John returned with the new farm machinery that ordinarily would have carried Father to heights of enthusiasm. John set in the pantry the barrels of sugar and kegs of molasses he had brought, but Mother had no time for fancy cooking.

Supplies were going out so fast that John soon again prepared to take the pack train to Lapwai for more. He and his Indian helpers were ready to start one morning when Mother came out to the yard, where Catherine and Elizabeth were seeing him off. Catherine thought she looked more worried than ever.

"John, please don't leave me," she begged. "Frank, Mary Ann, and Helen are all sick this morning. I'm sure it is measles. Father is worn out staying up so many nights in the Indian camp. I need you terribly."

John drew her into his arms. "Now, Mother, don't you worry. If you need me, of course I'll stay. My helpers can take the pack train to Lapwai, and Mr. Spalding can haul back the supplies. He is planning to bring Eliza for school, Father told me."

"Thank you, John." For a moment she rested in his arms, then hurried back to the house.

"I don't feel very well, either," Elizabeth whispered to Catherine.

"Neither do I. My throat hurts."

Before night, both were in bed, burning with fever, and soon John, Matilda, the Manson boys—everyone except Father and Mother—was down with measles. The sitting room and kitchen were full of beds, each holding a sick child, tossing and turning, crying out for water or complaining of headache. Father and Mother were here, there, and everywhere. If they slept, no one could tell when.

November was cold and rainy, and the two stoves, in the kitchen and sitting room, could warm only part of the house. Gradually, however, with the good care given them, the sick ones began to recover. Matilda, Frank, and David were soon bouncing around as lively as ever. John was well enough to help some in the house, though Father would not allow him to go outside in the cold. In the mansion house, most of the children felt fine, and Mother said she thought they could open the school the next Monday, November 29.

In the Indian camp, however, there was no improvement. In spite of Father's desperate efforts, people were dying at the rate of five or six a day, both children and adults. Some said almost half the tribe had been wiped out.

More than seventy people now lived at the mission—twenty-three in the main house, twenty-nine in the mansion house. Even the blacksmith shop had been turned into a dwelling, and twelve people lived at the sawmill in the mountains. Where had the happy life she had known disappeared, Catherine wondered. There was nothing now but sickness, death, and fear.

During this difficult time, Mr. Spalding arrived with his daughter Eliza. He said he would remain only a few days and at night could roll up in a blanket on the floor as he had done many a time. Eliza, on the other hand, would stay all winter, and somehow Mother squeezed in a cot for her.

A messenger, riding over from Umatilla, brought word that Five Crows, the one truly Christian chief of the Cayuse, who had been baptized by Mr. Spalding, wanted Father to visit his sick people.

"Come with me, Brother Spalding. The chief would be glad to see you again," Father urged.

They set off on horseback together the next morning, Friday, November 26, leaving Mother to care for the sick ones, most of whom were now on the mend. Catherine and Elizabeth, who shared the big bed in the sitting room, would soon be up again. Little Henrietta was also improving, but Helen and Louise seemed worse, if anything.

Mother was on her feet constantly from the time Father left until Sunday evening, when John said, "Go lie down for a while. Frank and I will stay up. If there is any change in the girls, we'll call you."

From her bed, Catherine watched Mother walk unsteadily from the room. She did not look like the strong, capable woman they had known these three years. Something terrible seemed about to happen. Catherine shivered and moved closer to Elizabeth.

"If only the Indians would stop that wailing," her sister groaned. Soon, however, she went to sleep, but Catherine could not. She jumped in terror when she heard the outside door open, but, seeing it was Father, she lay back, relieved. Now that he was here again, things would be better.

He looked exhausted, but before he would even sit down, he went the rounds of the beds, examining the children. Looking at Helen and Louise, he shook his head. "Boys, you might as well go to bed. I am going to sit up for a while," he said.

After John and Frank had gone upstairs, Mother came from her room to sit with him. Catherine heard him say in low tones that Stickus, his faithful friend who lived at Umatilla, had told him Joe Lewis was going from lodge to lodge, whipping up the Indians' anger. They were holding nightly councils planning when and where to kill him.

"Is this the end for us, Husband?"

"Somehow, I don't believe it. It is bad, but we have had bad times before and come out all right. We can only trust God and wait. Go back to bed, my dear. I 'll keep watch. I fear we cannot save these two." He gestured toward Helen and Louise."

After Mother had gone away, weeping, Catherine asked Father, "Are we all going to be killed?"

He came to sit on the edge of her bed and stroked her hair. "I don't think so, child. We still have some good friends among the Indians."

Soothed by his words, she drifted off to sleep.

When she woke, morning had come. Through the window in the sitting room door, she could see that the sky was dark and dreary, threatening rain. Elizabeth was already dressed and said she felt all well again. Catherine, too, felt well. She hurried into her clothes, and they went out to the kitchen.

Here in the warm room, bright with candlelight, Frank was setting the table and Father was cooking steak for breakfast. He said Mother was not feeling well and would stay in bed for a while. Matilda danced into the room, threw her arms around Father, and kissed him.

Then Eliza Spalding came in and, seeing Dr. Whitman, asked about her father.

"He did not come back with me," the doctor explained. "His horse fell on him and bruised his leg, but he will be all right. He will probably come tomorrow."

Elizabeth noticed the doctor dishing up the food. "Should I take some to Mother?"

"That would be a good idea." He filled a plate and she went off, holding it carefully. In a few minutes she was back. "Mother has been crying. But she said it was thoughtful of me to bring her the breakfast. I set the plate on the stand."

After they had finished eating, the girls began washing the dishes while Father talked with Mr. Rodgers about the trouble that seemed hanging over the mission.

"I'm going to do everything I can to please the Indians this winter," Father said. "If things are not better by spring, I shall move my family to The Dalles."

Just then, Mother came into the room looking calm again and more like herself As always, she was neatly dressed and had pinned her lovely bright hair back tightly. She did this every morning, though by noon some would be loosened from the knot at her neck and little wisps would be curling about her face. Catherine thought again how pretty she was.

"Judge Saunders told me yesterday he was ready to begin school today," she announced cheerfully. "The children have been unoccupied for so long that it will be good for all who are well enough to have something to do."

"Am I well enough?" Matilda asked.

"Yes, I think you and Frank, the Manson boys, and David are all well enough. And Eliza, of course. I hope you don't take the measles, Eliza, but I doubt if you will now."

"How about Elizabeth and me?" asked Catherine, who dearly loved school.

"No, I think you two and Mary Ann should wait a few more days," Mother replied. "The schoolroom is drafty, and you might take cold. Anyhow, you must have baths first. John, will you please bring the tub into the sitting room and set it beside the stove? Then I can keep watch of the sick children while I bathe the others."

Father stood up to leave, saying he had to go to an Indian child's funeral this morning. He wanted the parents to know he sympathized with them.

Mary Ann was first to have her bath. When she was dressed again, she went to the kitchen where John sat, watching a pot of meat cooking for dinner and keeping the fire going while he wound a hank of string into a ball. Broom-making was to be the next job, and it took a lot of string.

Matilda bounced into the kitchen for a drink of water.

"Hey, hold this hank for me, will you?" John asked.

"I can't. I'm only out for recess. I'll do it for you at noon." She dashed off again.

In the sitting room, Catherine finished her bath and began dressing; Elizabeth sat in the tub while Mother soaped her back. Father came in and dropped down in a chair near the stove.

"Cold out," he said, rubbing his hands. "A queer thing. Not many came to the funeral. But there seem to be more Indians around than usual."

"The men are butchering a cow this morning," Mother said. "The Indians always wait for their share."

At that moment a knock came at the closed door leading into the kitchen, and when Mother went to answer it, Catherine could see Tomahas standing there. This was unusual since the Indians were not supposed to come into the house. She heard a word or two exchanged, then Mother said, "Doctor, you are wanted."

Father went to the door, then turned. Catherine saw a strange look spread over his face. "Mother, bolt the door behind me."

Everything happened so fast that it was hard for Catherine to remember afterward just how it had been. She heard loud voices, a blow, a thud as of someone falling, John's cry that was quickly cut off. Then Mary Ann appeared at the front door. She had run all around the house from the kitchen. She was so terrified that she could hardly speak but managed to gasp, "The Indians are killing Father and John."

CHAPTER SEVENTEEN

The terrible day that Father had long feared but not actually expected had begun. Catherine sat stunned, one stocking halfway on. She saw that Mother, too, looked dazed. All the color left her cheeks; she walked up and down the room, wringing her hands and moaning, "My husband is killed and I am left a widow."

Then she noticed Elizabeth, still sitting in the tub of water. "Get dry and put on your clothes, child." As if moving in a dream, Elizabeth obeyed.

Women from the mansion house began pouring in at the side door, all, out of breath and white with terror. Mother recovered from her first shock and asked one of them to help her carry Father in from the kitchen. He was still breathing, and she bent over him, trying to stanch the blood pouring from a tomahawk wound in his head.

"Can you hear me, Marcus?"

His eyelids moved and his lips formed the word, "Yes."

"Can I do anything for you?"

"No." His eyes closed.

Mother clasped him in her arms as if hoping somehow to bring him back. Then she laid him down gently and pulled herself to her feet. Catherine noticed how her face had changed. Fear was gone. She lifted her head as if she were looking into the face of God, saying, "Lord, I am ready."

"Oh, Mother," Catherine thought, "how brave and wonderful you are; how much I love you." But there was no time to tell her. Mr. Rodgers and one of the immigrants, Mr. Kimball, rushed in. Mr. Rodgers was holding one arm; Mr. Kimball had a wound in his back. Mother came back to earth when she saw that both were bleeding. "Oh, that Joe Lewis! He is the one who started this. Our Indians never would have done it except for him."

Hoping to find out more of what was happening outside, she stepped briskly to a window, just as a bullet pierced the glass, shattering her shoulder. For a moment, she was stunned, then rallied to order, "We must all go upstairs." The other women rushed to help her. Mr. Rodgers and Mr. Kimball started up after them, but Catherine cried out, "Don't leave the sick children behind."

Mr. Rodgers scooped up Louise in his one good arm; Mr. Kimball managed to carry Helen and Henrietta. Upstairs, they laid the three on the bed beside Mother.

For a while, all was quiet. The frightened women and children had begun to hope the Indians had gone away when they heard steps below. A voice they recognized as that of Tamsucky, one of the chiefs, called that he was their friend and had come to help them. He offered safe conduct to the mansion house, saying that the Indians were going to burn this one. "I don't trust him," Mr. Rodgers said, but Mother differed. "God has raised us up a helper. I am willing to go if someone carries me. I am too weak to walk."

When she saw it was Joe Lewis who came up to help carry her, she hesitated, but it was too late. He lifted her over onto a cot and took one end, Mr. Rodgers the other. They started down the stairs, the women following. Catherine, Elizabeth, and Mary Ann stayed behind to comfort the three sick children, who alternately moaned and screamed. Mr. Kimball had rolled into a dark corner and did not move.

Catherine listened to the slow descent of the little procession down the stairs and through the sitting room where Father's body lay. She knew when they reached the kitchen. Then came the sounds of crashing furniture and dishes, yells, shots, and one awful cry from Mother. Catherine covered her face with her hands. Elizabeth crept close and whispered, "They killed her."

Gradually the sounds died away, followed by a silence that was even worse. Too terrified to move, the three girls sat on the floor beside the bed where the sick ones lay. Every moment Catherine expected to see Joe Lewis return, but the minutes and hours passed without another sound from below. Mary Ann went to sleep on the floor, but Catherine and Elizabeth sat close together, so frozen by fear that they could not even get up to see whether the sick ones were covered.

Once Elizabeth whispered, "John is dead. I wonder about Frank and Matilda."

"Maybe dead, too. Maybe we are the only ones left alive." Catherine put her arms around Elizabeth. "Mother was so brave; we must be brave, too."

"I don't feel brave."

"Neither do I."

Mr. Kimball, across the room, had stopped moaning, and the awful stillness was broken only by the snarl of cats fighting in the ravaged room below and the striking of Mother's wall clock. As the hours dragged by, Elizabeth found the clock's striking unendurable. She hid her head in Catherine's lap and stuffed her fingers in her ears but she could not keep out that sound.

Bong, bong. Two o'clock.

Hours, days, seemed to pass.

Bong, bong, bong. Three o'clock. Only three? Eternities dragged by.

Bong, bong, bong, bong. Elizabeth groaned, "I can't stand it." She turned away from her sister and sank into a fitful sleep. Catherine drew up her knees, folded her hands, and rested her head on them. Over and over in her mind went the events of the last few hours, like a nightmare. If only she might wake up and find it had never happened. She wished night would last forever or that the roof would fall in on them—anything to keep the Indians away.

When morning came, the sick children cried for water until Mr. Kimball could stand it no longer. He struggled up from the floor, wrapped a blanket around himself, and walked slowly down the stairs. The crackle of a gun out in the yard told Catherine the water would never come. After a while, she heard steps ascending the stairs. Joe Lewis and several Indians came in.

"You are not going to be hurt," Lewis said to the trembling girls. "Get your things together."

Catherine gathered up a few clothes and her two precious books, the family doctor book and Mama's Bible, but she could not carry them and one of the little sisters, too. The Indians told her they would bring her things later. She carried Louise, and Elizabeth picked up Henrietta, but when Mary Ann tried to lift Helen, she could not, and they had to leave her there, screaming.

"We'll come back for you," Catherine promised.

Somehow, they managed to get down the stairs, through those dreadful rooms, and along the familiar path to the mansion house. Some of the women met them, took their burdens, and led them inside. Laying Louise on a bed, Catherine sat down exhausted, but only until she had gotten her breath. Then, accompanied by two women, she went back for Helen. This time, when she reached the mansion house, she saw Matilda there with Eliza Spalding. They all fell into one another's arms.

"Where is Frank?" Catherine asked.

Matilda burst into sobs, so Eliza had to tell the story. At the first sound of gunfire, Judge Saunders, the teacher, rushed to the schoolroom door only to be shot down. Frank, the oldest boy in the room, decided the children should take refuge in the loft, and they piled books on a chair until he could reach the trapdoor opening. One by one, he boosted the children through it, then followed them.

"We must pray," he had said. Never, Eliza told Catherine, had she heard such wonderful prayers as Frank poured out. Soon they heard Joe Lewis calling from below that they should come down.

"You won't be hurt," he promised.

All but Frank went down to the yard where the Indians lined them up against the side of the house and discussed whether or not to shoot them. One of the older men said no, there had been enough killing.

After a while, Matilda was comforted to see Frank coming toward her. He took her hand and stood beside her, whispering, "I couldn't stay in the loft not knowing whether you had been killed."

Joe Lewis saw Frank, grabbed him by the shirt, and pulled him out of the line. "You bad boy," he said, and shot him through the head.

Women whose children had been in the schoolroom rushed to take them to the mansion house. Matilda and Eliza were left alone, too frightened to move or speak. All they

131

could do was wait, hand in hand. How long they stood there, freezing, they did not know. Finally, the man who had protested against any more killing came back, took them by the hand, and led them to the mansion house, where kind Mrs. Saunders, in spite of her own grief, drew them into her room, warmed them, and gave them something to eat.

Now began a month of terror for the women and children and the three men who had been spared to help the Indians. First of all, they took the two Manson boys and David Malin to Fort Walla Walla, saying they were part Indian, so were not to be hurt. For some unexplained reason, they did not feel the same about Mary Ann and Helen Mar, though Helen was too ill to have gone, even if they had suggested it.

She and Louise Sager, both unconscious part of the time, lay in one bed. Catherine sat beside them, giving them water and trying to soothe them. Louise moaned constantly, "John. I want Brother John."

Henrietta, however, was now able to be dressed, so Mrs. Saunders got up her courage to speak to one of the chiefs about the Sager children's clothing. All he brought them was one ragged blanket apiece and a few bits of Mrs. Whitman's underclothing, and someone had to lend them clothes after all.

Joseph Stanfield, one of the men left alive, was detailed to dig a grave for the victims, whose bodies still lay where they had fallen. Father Brouillet, the new Catholic priest, came over from the Umatilla to assist in this grim duty of giving the dead ones a decent burial. Trembling, Catherine held Henrietta, with Elizabeth and Matilda clinging to her on both sides, while the bodies, wrapped in sheets, were lowered into the long grave. Father and Mother lay at the end, then John and Frank, and the other ten who had died. None of the sisters cried; they could not believe those sheeted forms were really their parents and brothers. Only after the earth had been mounded over them did it come to Catherine that she was now the head of her family. As John had become a man the day their mother died, she now became a woman.

Life was so strange, she thought. If John had not been so kind to Mother, if he had gone to Lapwai with the pack train, he would be alive today. And if Frank had not come home that time he ran away, he, too, would still be living. Why was it that when one tried to do right, such terrible things could happen?

Two days later, Louise died; then Helen Mar and an immigrant child. The three were buried near the great mound, not far from Alice Whitman's grave, and Catherine felt comforted by the thought that Louise was with John.

In the days following the massacre, some of the young Indians, hysterical with excitement, looted the Whitman home, decking themselves out in Father's clothing and anything else that took their fancy. They soon discovered that the cellar was well stocked with food, and daily the Indians brought quantities of it to the mansion house to be cooked for them. Before each meal, they insisted on asking a blessing, using words that Mother and Father had taught them. After the prayer, some of the women must taste each dish in the presence of their captors to assure them nothing had been poisoned. Remembering Mother's comment on Mr. Gray's use of medicine to keep them away from his melons, Catherine understood their fear.

Turning to work as their one salvation, the women cooked extravagantly, even to making a batch of pies from dried peaches Mother had put away for a special occasion. Old Beardy, an ugly fellow, ate so much of the pie that he became very sick and raised the usual howl of poison. No one knew what might have happened if an Indian woman had not laughed and shamed him for being so greedy.

Next, the Indians brought bolts of calico from Mother's store and demanded that the women make them shirts. Every woman and girl who could hold a needle worked through the daylight hours and often by candlelight to finish the garments.

After a few days, Lorinda Bewley became very ill, and one of the women caring for her called Catherine aside. "We need some of Dr. Whitman's Number Six remedy. Could you go over to the house and bring a bottle from his medicine cabinet?" Evidently she saw the fear in Catherine's eyes. She said gently, "The Indians do not hurt children. If one of us women tried to go, they might kill us."

Catherine held in her quivering stomach and said, "I'll go."

"Walk. If you run, they will chase you."

Catherine stepped out of the mansion house. Not an Indian was in sight, but she knew they were watching her from their hiding places. Never had a road looked so long as the path leading to the wrecked Whitman home. She began to count steps: "One, two, three—" then ten steps, twenty, fifty, a hundred.

She looked neither to the right nor the left but kept her eyes steadily on the green door that had opened so long ago to welcome her in to love and care. Two hundred steps, two hundred and fifty. She was over the threshold. She could not bear to look at the smashed table and chairs, the beautiful Spode dishes lying in a broken pile on the floor, but walked straight to the medicine cabinet, saw the bottle with "No. 6" on the label, reached for it—

"What you do?" A rough voice stopped her. A hand gripped her shoulder. She held up her head as Mother would have done. "Medicine for a sick child."

The hand fell from her shoulder. She slipped the bottle into her dress pocket, turned, and walked out, slow step after slow step, her heart pounding, throat dry, every nerve in her body urging, "Run! Run!" but she did not run. Now she knew how many steps she would need to reach safety. At two hundred she could hardly hold her feet in their slow pace; at two hundred and twenty-five she stopped trying. In a bold dash, she reached the door.

"You are a brave girl," the women said, hugging her.

"I told an Indian a lie. I said it was medicine for a sick child."

A swift hug was the reply.

Indian women, their faces wet with tears, began bringing to the mansion house things their men had stolen, including Mama's Bible and Papa's doctor book. Old Stickus, Father's friend, also came weeping. "We have killed our best friends."

Frank's death seemed to prey on the minds of the Indian boys, who told Catherine he came back to them in their dreams. Only a few, though, seemed really to regret what they had done, and almost every day, some young fellow told the women that if American soldiers came up from the Willamette Valley, all the captives would be killed. Maybe they would be killed anyhow. In the Indians' changeable mood, anything could happen.

In spite of their growing fear that soldiers might come and thereby cause their deaths, the captives occasionally found something amusing that, for a moment, lifted the pall that hung over them. One day an Indian rode up with a peculiar-looking saddleblanket on his horse, and the children had to laugh when they recognized it as the fine big map of the world Father had bought for the schoolroom.

Relief of another kind came when one of the women cautiously opened the door in answer to a knock, and Eliza

Spalding rushed through to throw herself into the arms of the Indian who stood there. He was Timothy, a Nez Percé, who had been Mr. Spalding's first convert and a faithful friend to the white men ever since.

"Are all my family dead?" Eliza asked when she had brought him inside.

"No, little Eliza, they are all safe. Your father was on his way to Waiilatpu when he heard that the doctor and his wife had been murdered and he would be too if he went on to the mission. He had a hard time reaching Lapwai, traveling at night and hiding in the daytime, but he made it. Now I have come to take you home, if the Cayuse will permit."

For a day, Eliza hoped against hope, but the word was no. Timothy had to leave without her. "Keep up your courage. We are all praying for you. You shall see your parents again," he assured her.

The Cayuse said they could not let her go because they needed her for an interpreter. Mother's store of flour had been used up, and they did not know how to run the gristmill. They had spared the miller, but since he knew no Cayuse, they could not talk to him. They were aware that Eliza spoke their language and demanded that she go to the mill to interpret for them. Eliza looked wildly around the circle of women and children. Their eyes pleaded with her. She turned to her best friend, "Elizabeth, will you go with me?"

Now it was Elizabeth's turn to look around the circle of pleading eyes. She drew in her breath. "I'll go."

The day was cold, the wind biting. The girls put on their ragged coats and carried a blanket to the mill, where they were told they must stay all day. Between spurts of Eliza's interpreting, they dug a hole in a straw stack that stood near and crawled into it to get out of the wind. Every few minutes an Indian jerked Eliza from the hole to tell the miller what he wanted done, but when he had finished, he let her crawl in with Elizabeth again. After several days of rough treatment the Indians could indicate with signs what they wanted of the miller, and the girls were left alone.

One morning a whisper went around the mansion house, "Today is Christmas." In the misery of the captives' lives, the thought of Christmas brought a moment of happiness as the women hunted through their personal possessions for any little things they could give the children for presents. They went upstairs to one of the rooms farthest from the Indians and prepared a small treat of dried fruits and bread spread with hoarded jelly. For each child there was a handkerchief or small book. To the Sager girls, who had not celebrated Christmas for three years, it was wonderful.

By now, the captives felt it had been a lifetime since they were free. Then, on the day after Christmas, a swift rider came with the incredible news, "Uncle Pete has bought you from the Indians."

"Who is Uncle Pete?" the children wanted to know. "Peter Skene Ogden, of the Hudson's Bay Company, down at Fort Vancouver," was the answer.

"Thank God, he has come to rescue us!" The chiefs sulkily gave the order, "You go in three days."

On the morning of December 29, one month after the massacre, the three wagons that had not been destroyed headed westward toward Fort Walla Walla, twenty-five miles away. Each person was allowed to take only one small bundle of clothing and one blanket, but Catherine managed to hang on to her two precious books.

Stickus, who had opposed the massacre, and Old Beardy, who was perhaps ashamed of his adventure with the peach pies, rode beside the last wagon, in which the Sager girls sat, as escort in case any of the wild young men should change their minds. Even so, as they rode through the Indian camp, a woman ran out, calling, "Hurry, hurry. They get you yet." The driver laid on the whip, but the oxen could go only so fast.

Darkness was closing in when the survivors saw in the distance the huge, dark bulk of the fort, passed through its great gate, and knew they were safe. Only then did the terrible day that had begun a month before really end.

CHAPTER EIGHTEEN

Catherine and her sisters climbed stiffly out of the wagon and looked around. They could not yet believe they were safe. Mrs. Saunders, who had ridden with them, led them across an open courtyard to a candlelit room where several men were sitting.

Matilda, eyes wide, walked straight to a white-haired stranger. "Are you Uncle Pete?"

He bent toward her. "What did you say, little girl?"

"Are you Uncle Pete, the man who bought us from the Indians? If you are, I want to thank you."

"That pays me well." Peter Skene Ogden laughed and set her on his knee. From that moment, she became his special pet.

The four girls were most tenderly cared for. Everyone seemed to realize that of all the captives, they had suffered the most. Many of the women had lost their husbands but still had their children; the children had lost their fathers, but their mothers were still with them. The Sager girls had lost their second set of parents, both brothers and one sister. What was to become of them, no one yet could tell, for they had no known relatives.

On the following day, when the chiefs came to collect the ransom, the captives learned that the price of their freedom had been 62 three-point Hudson's Bay blankets, 63 cotton shirts, 12 guns, 600 loads of ammunition, 12 flints, and 37 pounds of tobacco—worth altogether about five hundred dollars.

The Sager girls were delighted to find Mr. Stanley, the artist, here. He told them he had been on his way to Waiilatpu the day of the massacre when his Spokane Indian guide had learned the terrible news from a passing acquaintance. Stanley had stopped at the fort while the guide hurried back to tell the Eells and Walkers.

Mr. Ogden sent word to the Spalding family to come, and anxious days followed while those in the fort waited for them to arrive. Some of the young Cayuse had bragged that Mr. Spalding would never get there alive. They had not counted on the devotion of the Nez Percés, who had formed a bodyguard to surround Mr. and Mrs. Spalding, their three young children, and Mary Johnson. The day they reached the fort, a shout of relief went up from those inside, especially Eliza.

It had been decided that from Fort Walla Walla the survivors would travel down the Columbia River to Fort Vancouver, and while waiting for the Spaldings, the women had made good use of their time to bake quantities of bread and cook pots of meat for the trip.

At dawn on Monday, January 3, 1848, the Hudson's Bay men lined up their three large bateaux at the edge of the river. Each boat could carry fifteen to twenty passengers and eight paddlers. The former captives hurried down from the fort and took their places while armed men stood on guard.

The Manson boys were going to their father in Vancouver, but David Malin would have to stay behind.

Mr. McBean, the new Hudson's Bay factor, said because the boy was an Indian, not a member of Dr. Whitman's family, there would be no one in the valley to take charge of him. As the boats shot out into the current of the mighty Columbia, Catherine and her sisters looked back to see him standing alone on the shore, crying as if his heart would break. The girls felt that they had lost another brother.

Uncle Pete had assigned the Sager girls and Mr. Stanley to his own bateau. Together, the two men struggled to keep the children as comfortable as possible. Mr. Ogden, a big, jolly fellow, told stories of his adventures to take their minds off the dangers that still haunted them, both from Indians and from the river itself. The higher the waves and wind, the louder he laughed and the faster he talked.

Mr. Stanley kept Matilda and Elizabeth on the thwart beside him, with his own blanket wrapped around them on top of theirs. Even so, they ached with cold long before Mr. Ogden ordered the boats ashore for the night. As soon as they set foot on land, the men hurried up the bank to set up tents and start fires.

Though Henrietta was only three and a half years old and thin from her illness, she was a heavy load for Catherine as she struggled out of the boat. Suddenly, she felt the child lifted from her arms. Uncle Pete handed her his gun holster. "You be my armor-bearer and I'll carry the baby."

Catherine laughed for the first time that day. From then on, this was the procedure every time they went ashore.

After a quick supper, everyone crawled into the tents for shelter from the bitter wind and bedded down as best they could. Again, Mr. Stanley came to the aid of the Sager girls, giving them his blanket.

"How will you keep warm?" Catherine asked him.

"Oh, I'll bunk with Uncle Pete. He is fat enough to keep both of us at the boiling point." His jolly laugh reassured the shivering girls.

On the afternoon of the sixth day, the boatmen suddenly began to sing and paddle with great speed. The refugees, who had been huddling silently together, sat up as if new life had been poured into them. Along the shore they saw a great

141

crowd of men, waving their hats and yelling as the boats swung in to the beach. Fort Vancouver! The great fort of which Father and Mother had so often spoken. The girls marveled at the high walls, the bastions at the corners, and the British Union Jack flying above the main building.

Two days later, the drab little party again took to the boats to cross the Columbia and paddle a short distance up the Willamette River to the new city of Portland. There, about fifty Oregon Volunteers were camped across the river, and as the canoes appeared, the soldiers fired a salute. At the first shot, the Sager girls dropped to the bottom of the boat, sure they were yet to be killed, but Mr. Stanley bent over them. "It's all right, little ones. They are just welcoming you."

The children could now see some of the soldiers getting into boats to cross over to them. Catherine recognized General Cornelius Gilliam, who had been with their wagon train and now was leader of the Volunteers. He leaped to the dock and hurried to the girls, standing beside Mr. Ogden. "I want to shake hands with my young friends, the Sager girls. I remember your parents well," he said to the comfort of Catherine in particular. To think that someone here knew them!

To their surprise, Captain Shaw, their old friend, was there also with three of his sons, all members of the Volunteers. Everywhere were smiling faces, making the girls feel less alone.

They met Governor Abernethy, who had once been a missionary and knew the Whitmans, and he invited the Spaldings and the Sager girls to stay at his home in Oregon City, a few miles upstream, for a day or two. Mr. Stanley had hurried away without saying good-bye. Catherine felt a little hurt about it but soon saw him coming back along the rough street, carrying several packages.

"Now then, my little friends, I want you to have something to remember me by." He gave one package to each girl. "Don't open them now, but when you get to your new home, wherever it may be, you will find enough cloth in each package for a new dress."

"Oh, thank you, Mr. Stanley," they shouted. New dresses! Did anyone ever need them more!

"Come, children," Mr. Spalding called. "The governor's boat is waiting."

The girls clambered over the side of the canoe with the Spaldings and the governor. Two men paddled it up the river until they came in sight of a magnificent waterfall where the Willamette River poured over great rock ledges. At one side, a small town had grown up with houses both above and below the falls: Oregon City, capital of the provisional territory.

They walked up the rough street, Eliza Spalding with her family and the Sager girls lagging behind, so tired they could hardly walk. The others reached the governor's house and climbed a short flight of steps to the open door where his wife waited to greet them. Catherine heard the voices, then the door closed. She and her sisters seemed to have been forgotten.

At the foot of the steps they stood in a forlorn little group, Henrietta leaning against Catherine, Matilda and Elizabeth beside her. From the river below them rose a thick, cold fog; the roar of the falls sounded like thunder. All around stood a forest of fir trees, so tall they seemed to pierce the sky. A damp, pungent odor assailed the girls' nostrils. As the short January day waned, darkness came down upon them, broken only here and there by the feeble light of a candle in houses they could not see.

Matilda and Elizabeth began to cry softly, their tears making cold, wet spots in Catherine's ragged dress. An awful feeling of desolation swept over her. Never, in all the terrible weeks behind them, had she felt so utterly alone.

Mental pictures flashed across her mind—Papa's burial place beside the Green River, Mama's at Pilgrim Springs. That dreadful long grave at Waiilatpu where John and Frank lay, Louise all by herself. Oh, why had they ever left Missouri? Or why had they not all died at Waiilatpu? At least, they would have been together, she thought, and wished she could lie down here and never get up again.

Then, somehow, like a flower pushing its way up through frozen earth, a memory grew and bloomed in her mind. As clearly as if it were happening right now, she heard voices: "Are we children stout-hearted, Papa?"

"Of course. All the Sagers have been stout-hearted or Great-Grandfather would never have got to Germany or Grandfather to the United States or my father to Ohio or we to Missouri. We'll have to be stout-hearted to get to Oregon, but we will."

At the head of the steps, the door opened and the governor's wife called, "You girls must be getting cold out there. Come on in. You can see Oregon tomorrow." Catherine felt wild delirious joy sweep through her. "Elizabeth! Matilda! Henrietta! Stop that crying! We're in Oregon! We got here!"

She felt her sisters relax, felt the answering joy that straightened their drooping bodies.

"Oregon! We're in Oregon!" they shrieked.

Hand in hand, laughing through their tears, the four of them marched up the steps into their new life.

WHAT HAPPENED AFTERWARD

It would be comforting to think that the troubles of the surviving Sager girls were now over, that kind friends took them in and kept them together as the Whitmans had done, but this did not happen. The Oregon settlers were mostly poor, struggling, and plentifully supplied with children of their own. A family might take in one child but not four. Consequently, the Sager girls were separated and never lived together as a family again.

They accepted this situation with the same courage they had always shown. In their separate homes they went to school whenever there was a chance, worked hard, had a few good times, and married young.

None of them ever held any resentment toward Indians. As they grew up, they came to understand the causes of the massacre. First, the Indians felt the incoming white settlers threatened their homes; then the tragic deaths of so many Indian children from measles and the false stories spread by Joe Lewis so upset and inflamed them that the desperate, grieving red men had killed people who were trying to be their friends.

Henrietta, youngest of the girls, had no children and died at the age of twenty-six after being mistakenly shot by a desperado in the mining town where she and her husband were living. The other three sisters all raised large families:

Catherine and Matilda had eight children each and Elizabeth nine. Their descendants are scattered up and down the Pacific Coast and into the Midwest.

As time passed, Catherine realized that she and her sisters had lived through an important period of American history that should be recorded by someone who had been on the scene. Therefore, almost ten years after coming to Oregon, she wrote a detailed account of the family's journey across the plains, of their life at the Whitman Mission, of the massacre and their final journey to Oregon. Catherine hoped to see it in book form and even dreamed that it might make enough money to set up an orphanage in memory of Narcissa Whitman. She was never able to find a publisher, but her story, carefully preserved by her children and grandchildren, is one of the most authentic sources of information about that tragic episode and is constantly used by historians and researchers.

Eventually, the three girls did hear from relatives. One uncle and his family moved to California and once visited Catherine in Oregon.

On the fiftieth anniversary of the Whitman Massacre, the three sisters were invited to be honored guests at the dedication of a monument on the site of the mission. It stands there today, a tall marble shaft like a finger pointing to the sky, on the hill above the beautiful valley the girls had all come to love. In 1940, the grounds and the great grave, now covered with a marble slab containing the names of those who died on that terrible day, became the Whitman Mission National Historic Site, visited by thousands of tourists every year.

The three sisters all lived to a good old age. Catherine and her husband, Clark Pringle, spent their later years in the home of their youngest child, Lucia Pringle Collins, in Spokane,

Washington, where she passed away August 10, 1910, at the age of seventy-five. Elizabeth died on July 19, 1925, in Portland, Oregon, a few days after her eighty-eighth birthday. Matilda, last of the original Sager family, was living with a daughter in California when she died on April 13, 1928, aged eighty-nine.

The participants in this story were not without their faults. Many things they said and did, in the light of today's understanding, seem to have been mistaken. But of their courage and devotion to duty as they saw it, there can be no question. They were truly stout-hearted folk.